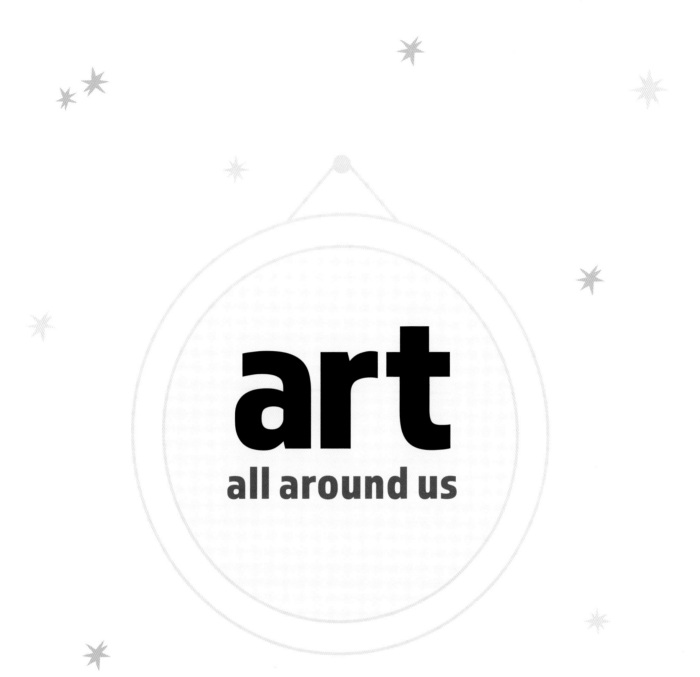

art
all around us

art
all around us

A Kid's Guide to
Finding Art in Everyday Life

Xiao Situ

union
square
kids

NEW YORK

union square kids
NEW YORK

UNION SQUARE KIDS and the distinctive Union Square Kids logo are trademarks of Union Square & Co.

Union Square & Co., LLC, is a subsidiary of Sterling Publishing Co., Inc.

First Union Square Kids edition published in the United States and Canada in 2024.

This book was designed and produced by Quarto Publishing, an imprint of The Quarto Group, One Triptych Place, London, SE1 9SH, United Kingdom.

ISBN 978-1-4549-5526-9 (hardcover)
ISBN 978-1-4549-5527-6 (e-book)

For information about custom editions, special sales, and premium purchases, please contact specialsales@unionsquareandco.com.

Printed in China

10 9 8 7 6 5 4 3 2 1

05/24

unionsquareandco.com

CONTENTS

INTRODUCTION: **CIRCLES OF ART**   8

CHAPTER 1 **SELF** 13

Mirror, Mirror 14

Elisabeth Louise Vigée Le Brun,
   Julie Louise Le Brun Looking in a Mirror 16

Figurine of a Girl with a Mirror 17

Mirror 18

Hair Comb Decorated with Rows of Wild Animals 19

Self-Portraits and Self-Fashioning 20

Sofonisba Anguissola, *Self-Portrait at the Easel* 22

Judith Leyster, *Self-Portrait* 23

George Bellows, *Lady Jean* 24

"Smiling" Figure 25

Portrait Vessel of a Ruler 26

Amy Sherald,
   He Was Meant for All Things to Meet 27

Dress Sewn by Rosa Parks 28

Coty L'Aimant 29

Locket with Photographs of Harriette and
   Harry T. Moore 30

Pair of Ear Ornaments with Winged Runners 31

Guanyin of the Southern Sea 32

Mickalene Thomas, *Portrait of Mnonja* 33

CHAPTER 2 **HOME AND FAMILY** 35

Family Portraits 36

Portrait of the Situ Family 38

Kehinde Wiley, *Portrait of Asia-Imani,
   Gabriella-Esnae, and Kaya Palmer* 39

Florine Stettheimer, *Family Portrait, II* 40

James Van Der Zee, *Wedding Day, Harlem* 41

Home Activities 42

Sleeping Lady 44

Mary Cassatt, *Little Girl in a Blue Armchair* 45

Pierre Bonnard, *The Yellow Shawl* 46

Wada Sanzo, Title Unknown
   (Four Children Playing a Game) 47

Home Furnishings 48

Parein Biscuit Tin 50

Doña Rosa Solís y Menéndez,
   Embroidered Coverlet (Colcha) 51

Worktable 52

Bowl with Children in a Garden 53

Handle Spout Vessel with Relief Depicting a
   Standing Figure, Holding Farming Tools 54

Sam Buganski, *Malibu Mug* 55

CHAPTER 3 **COMMUNITY** 57

Teaching and Learning........................58

Seated Adult and Youth.........................60

Henry Ossawa Tanner, *The Banjo Lesson* 61

Martha Perkins, Sampler 62

Headdress (Chi Wara) 63

Nizami, *Laila and Majnun in School* 64

Starfield Library, Seoul 65

Faith Ringgold, *Dancing at the Louvre* 66

Raphael Soyer, *Dancing Lesson* 67

Being Together.....................................68

Bayeux Tapestry 70

Maharana Jagat Singh Attending the Raslila 71

Model of a Ballgame with Spectators.........................72

Panel from a Casket with Scenes from
Courtly Romances 73

Funerary Relief of a Vegetable Vendor.........................74

John Heywood, *Miss Harrison's Sweet Shop:
House of Nectar* 75

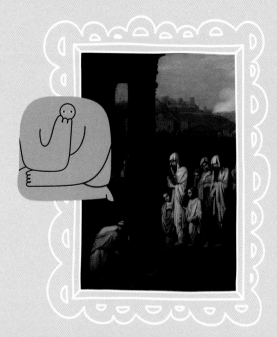

CHAPTER 4 **SOCIETY** 77

Many Communities, One Society...................78

Gordon Parks, *Untitled* 80

Benton Spruance, *The People Work—Evening*..........8

Benjamin West, *Agrippina Landing at
Brundisium with the Ashes of Germanicus* 82

Bronislaw Bak, *Parade,* from *One-Hundred
Views of Chicago* 83

Great Mosque of Djenné, Mali................84

Colosseum, Rome 85

Built Environments 86

Shibam, Yemen.......................................88

Machu Picchu, Peru 89

Yin Xiuzhen, *Portable City: Hangzhou* 90

Mohamad Hafez, *Unsettled Nostalgia* 91

Little Island, New York City.....................92

Lumphini Park, Bangkok 93

Jean Tinguely and Niki de Saint Phalle,
Stravinsky Fountain 94

Si-o-se-pol (Allahverdi Khan Bridge), Isfahan 95

Ernest Zacharevic, *Little Children on a Bicycle* 96

Elizabeth Catlett, *Students Aspire* 97

CHAPTER 5 **NATURE** 99

CHAPTER 6 **COSMOS** 123

Ecosystems 100

Maize God Emerging from a Flower 102

Georgia O'Keeffe, *The Lawrence Tree* 103

Utagawa Hiroshige, *Sudden Shower over
Shin-Ōhashi Bridge and Atake* 104

Emily Kame Kngwarreye, *Earth's Creation* 105

Mask 106

Basawan and Dharmdas, *Akbar* 107

Grandma Moses, *Grandma Moses Goes
to the Big City* 108

Morgain Bailey, *Mississippi Mud* 109

Inspired by Nature 110

Great Serpent Mound, Peebles, Ohio 112

Fire Flame Cooking Vessel (Ka'en Doki) 113

Birds and Flowers of the Four Seasons 114

Cloud-Collar Pillow with Waves 115

Wine Jar with Fish and Aquatic Plants 116

Lion Cub 117

Berndnaut Smilde, *Nimbus* Installations 118

North Wind Mask (Negakfok) 119

Wenzel Friedrich, *Fancy Chair No. 7* 120

Meret Oppenheim, *Object
(Le Déjeuner en fourrure)* 121

Origin Stories 124

Giovanni di Paolo, *The Creation of the
World and the Expulsion from Paradise* 126

Zakariya ibn Muhammad al-Qazwini,
The Angel Ruh Holding the Celestial Spheres 127

Geo Soctomah Neptune, *Apikcilu Binds the Sun* .. 128

Wheel of Life 129

Stargazing 130

Ellen Harding Baker, *Solar System* Quilt 132

Joseph Wright of Derby, *A Philosopher
Giving a Lecture on the Orrery* 133

Margaret Nazon, *Night Sky* 134

Cosmic Cliffs 135

Cosmic Imagination 136

Hugh Ferriss, *Philosophy* 138

Wangechi Mutu, *In Two Canoe* 139

GLOSSARY 140

INDEX 142

CREDITS & ACKNOWLEDGMENTS 144

INTRODUCTION:
Circles of Art

What are your earliest memories of art? Perhaps it was using finger paints or crayons to make a picture, or molding clay into different shapes. Maybe it was inserting beads onto string to create jewelry, or dipping fabric into dyes to make colorful clothing. Or was it gluing feathers to a mask, or adding sequins to a piece of fabric?

How did you know that what you were doing was art? Was it because it involved you choosing different colors, using your hands, and making creative decisions? Or was it because it felt engaging as you were making it and looked pleasing when it was done? Or did you know because somebody told you that it was art and proudly displayed it on a wall after you were finished? Where did your understanding of what art is come from?

The definition of art has changed throughout human history and varies across different cultures around the world. When most people today hear the word "art," they think about the paintings and sculptures in a museum. But this idea of art as objects that are set apart from everyday life and displayed in a special building is relatively new—just a few hundred years old! For hundreds of thousands of years before that, art was everywhere, and lots of things were considered art.

Objects that people had in their homes and handled on a daily basis counted as art—things like baskets, bowls, blankets,

and furniture. Ornaments and utensils used for cultural ceremonies or religious rituals were also considered art, as well as the jewelry, clothing, and accessories that people wore for special occasions. Many of these items are now stored and displayed in museums as art, but before that they were still active in people's everyday lives, available for them to touch, use, and appreciate in a more common way. People created these objects to express who they were and what was important to them.

ABOUT THIS BOOK

This book encourages you to look all around you to notice artistic qualities in the things you see and use every day. This includes the clothing and accessories you wear, the family photos and decorative fabrics that adorn your home, and the parks and public spaces you spend time in. When you start thinking about these things as art, you'll begin seeing the beauty in them and appreciate how much they tell you about who you are, the places you live, and how you're connected to others.

This Greek sculpture called *Winged Victory of Samothrace* is now in a museum, but thousands of years ago it was made as an offering (holy gift) to be displayed in a sanctuary (holy place).

This book imagines the world around you as six concentric circles, each one wider and more inclusive of other people, communities, and spaces than the one before. It starts with the self (that's you!), then moves on to home and family, then to community, society, nature, and, finally, the cosmos.

When a baby is born, most of what they experience of the world is centered on their own needs and the protective environment of their home and family. As they grow, their world widens to include more people and places. At every stage, the objects that surround you help you to explore your role and purpose in each circle of space. All the artworks included in each chapter help you to do that.

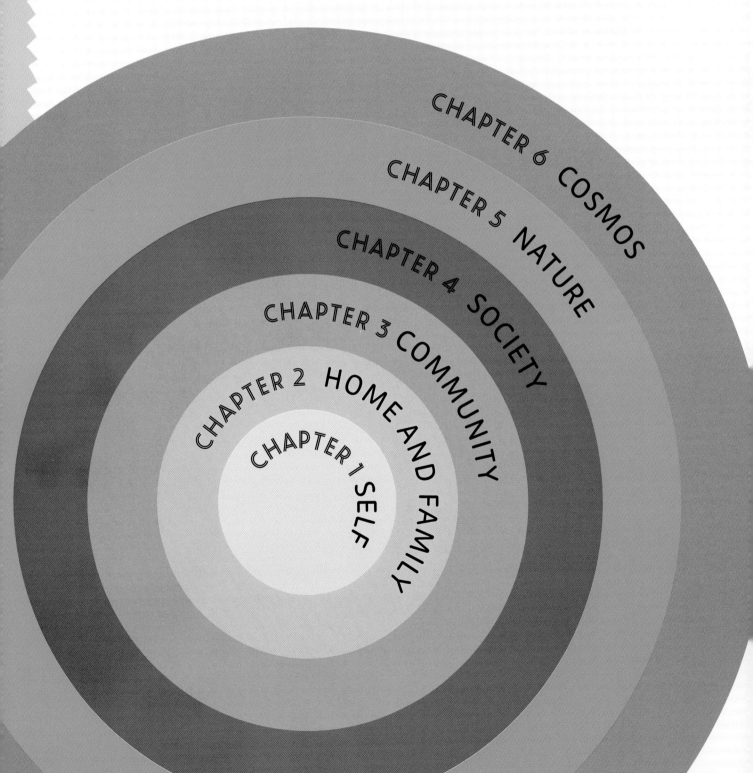

CHAPTER 6 COSMOS

CHAPTER 5 NATURE

CHAPTER 4 SOCIETY

CHAPTER 3 COMMUNITY

CHAPTER 2 HOME AND FAMILY

CHAPTER 1 SELF

Shoes are accessories we wear every day, but they can be artistic objects too. Choosing how to design a pair of shoes and what kinds to wear can be a form of creative expression.

As an **art historian**, I have spent a lot of time looking at and thinking about the art stored and displayed in museums. The more I learn about and teach with these art objects, the more I realize that they are not so different from the common items that surround people in their everyday lives today.

One of the most important lessons I've learned from the work I do is that the more we consider the common things around us as art, the more beauty and meaning we discover they have, and the more we can appreciate them and take care of them now, right where we are.

This leads to a wider and more expansive definition of art. Art doesn't have to be set apart and kept in a special place where you get to see it only once in a while. If something involves thought, care, skill, interest, beauty, or meaning, then it counts as art. Art is all around you, all the time—you just need to start looking!

CHAPTER 1

SELF

People are always interested in images (pictures) of themselves. Your image might be a selfie, a photograph, or another kind of art. It can show other people what you look like, how you feel, or what's important to you. You can also use clothing, accessories, and makeup to express how you feel. You can style your hair or decorate your body to match your look to your mood.

MIRROR, MIRROR

Your reflection is the image you see of yourself when you look in a mirror to brush your teeth, comb your hair, or try on new outfits. When you see your reflection, do you make different facial expressions or try out interesting poses? Playing with your reflection can help you be creative with how you look and feel.

NOT A DRAWING

This Japanese artwork is a **woodblock print**. To create this, an artist starts with a block of wood. They use sharp tools to carve a picture onto one side. Next, they apply ink onto the carved surface and press a sheet of paper onto the ink. The picture then appears on the paper. This allows an artist to make many copies, known as **prints**, of the image.

When a woodblock print has just one color, only one block of wood is needed. When it has different colors (like this image), different parts of the image are divided onto multiple blocks. Each piece gets a different color ink that gets printed onto the paper, producing a multicolor image. For this print, Kitagawa Utamaro also applied a shiny material called **mica** onto the surface. This makes it sparkle like a mirror!

GETTING READY

What do you think the woman is getting ready to do? Is she dressing up to meet friends or washing her face after a big day? What makes you think that?

The woman has a fancy hairstyle. Notice all her bows and clips! She can see just the front of her hairstyle, but we can see the back too. Which accessory can we see that the woman *cannot* see in her reflection? Why might it be important to her that other people can see the back of her hairdo, even if she can't?

Kitagawa Utamaro, Naniwa Okita Admiring Herself in a Mirror, made around 1790–95 (woodblock print)

Elisabeth Louise Vigée Le Brun,
Julie Louise Le Brun Looking in a Mirror

The girl in this painting was the artist's daughter, Julie. Throughout Julie's childhood, her mother, Elisabeth, painted her portrait many times. In some paintings, Julie is shown hugging Elisabeth. Here, Julie is alone. Her mother was a favorite artist of the king and queen of France during the 1700s and 1800s. She painted many portraits of royalty.

IMAGINE

NOT ONCE, BUT TWICE

Elisabeth painted Julie's face from two angles: from the side, and from the front as a reflection in the mirror. How does seeing Julie from two viewpoints make us think about her differently?

WHAT'S SHE THINKING?
Julie seems to be thinking as she looks into the mirror. What would you write inside a thought bubble?

made around 1787

Figurine of a Girl with a Mirror

To make this ancient Greek sculpture, the artist first used their fingers to mold a lump of soft clay into the shape they wanted. Once they were happy with how the shape looked, it was placed in a special oven called a **kiln**. The heat in the kiln "cooked" the clay until it turned into a hard material called **terra-cotta**. Once the sculpture came out, it was solid and could no longer be changed.

made around 320–270 BCE

THINK ABOUT

MONSTER MIRROR

You may not be able to see it here, but the mirror the girl is holding is decorated with an image of Medusa. In Greek myth, Medusa was a monster with snakes growing from her head instead of hair. Whoever looked Medusa in the eyes turned to stone! Why do you think the artist chose to show Medusa on the mirror?

MULTICOLORED

This sculpture was originally painted in different colors. Which colors would you use for each part?

Mirror

A long time ago, people only saw their reflections in pools or bowls of water. When people started making tools, they hammered metal into flat sheets. These were the first mirrors! As mirrors became more common, people thought about the way they looked and explored ways of expressing themselves through their appearance. When someone looked into this ancient Egyptian mirror, they could see their reflection above the goddess's head. Maybe this made them feel special!

THINK ABOUT

BURIED TREASURE

In ancient Egypt, lots of beautiful belongings, including this mirror, were put into tombs with the dead. What does this say about how people thought of the afterlife?

SECRET TOOL

Do you notice the small hole above the goddess's head? Inside, there is a little peg that holds the two separate pieces of the mirror together—the circular part and the handle.

made around 1492–1472 BCE

Hair Comb Decorated with Rows of Wild Animals

This ancient Egyptian sculpture is a comb! Can you believe it? There used to be teeth on the bottom, but over time they broke off. It was probably used for special occasions, since the top part is so carefully decorated with many kinds of animals. The artist didn't want you to just use the comb to fix your hair. They also wanted you to look closely at the animals.

made around 3200–3100 BCE

LOOK CLOSELY

ANIMAL PARADE

There are many animals carved onto this comb. How many kinds can you name? Which animals are facing left and which are heading right? Does each row have a mix of different types of animals, or are they all the same kind?

SPECIAL MATERIAL

This comb is carved from a hard, white material called **ivory**. It comes from the teeth (tusks) of large animals like elephants. In modern times, it has often been unlawfully obtained and sold.

SELF-PORTRAITS AND SELF-FASHIONING

Do you like to choose what to wear? Do you enjoy picking out accessories like bags, hats, or scarves? We often like to wear certain things because they look good or express how we feel inside, making us feel special, creative, or talented. When we make decisions about what to wear or how we look, it's called **self-fashioning** or **self-expression**. When you make art that shows yourself the way you want to look, it's called a **self-portrait**.

SO MANY SELF-PORTRAITS!

During her lifetime, Mexican artist Frida Kahlo painted over fifty self-portraits in different moods and settings. In some, she's in a forest surrounded by birds or monkeys. In others, she's lying on a bed looking sad or sick. Sometimes, she painted herself with short hair, wearing a man's suit.

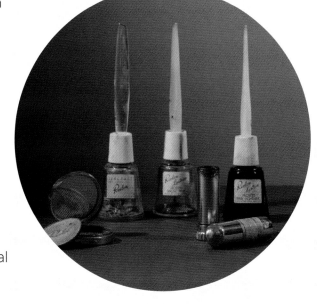

In this self-portrait, Frida is in a forest filled with leaves, twigs, and flower buds. The sky is gray and stormy. Her hair is gathered into a twisted updo, adorned with flowers. She's also wearing an earring shaped like a hand and a necklace of thorns that cuts her skin. In the white banner, Frida writes in Spanish that she's dedicating this painting to Leo Eloesser, her good friend and trusted doctor. He once cared for her at the hospital when her leg was hurting.

REVEALING FEELINGS

Frida's self-portraits showed on the outside what she was feeling on the inside. Look closely at the artist's facial expression and accessories, and at the setting. How would you describe what she might be feeling inside?

Frida was creative with her clothing, hairstyle, and makeup. She liked that she had a slight mustache and that her eyebrows connected in the middle. Sometimes she used makeup to make the hairs darker. The cosmetics shown above belonged to the artist. Can you spot where on Frida's face she would have applied each type of makeup?

Frida Kahlo, *Self-Portrait Dedicated to Dr. Eloesser,*

made around 1940 (oil on masonite)

Sofonisba Anguissola, *Self-Portrait at the Easel*

In this self-portrait, Italian artist Sofonisba Anguissola (*so-fuh-NEES-buh ang-gwee-SOH-luh*) shows herself painting a mother hugging her child. This artist painted many portraits of the king and queen of Spain during the 1500s and was also their kids' tutor. She got to live in their palace! She wanted to show that she was dedicated to her role as an artist, teacher, and caregiver to the royal family. What clues do you see that show this?

TRY IT OUT

MATCHING GAME

Look closely at the artist's **palette**. Can you match each paint color to where it's used in the painting? Is there a color in the painting that's missing from the palette? Did Sofonisba have to mix any colors?

made around 1556

HELPFUL TOOL
The longer stick that the artist is using is called a **maulstick**. It helps keep her hand still so it doesn't shake when she's painting.

Judith Leyster, *Self-Portrait*

This self-portrait shows Dutch artist Judith Leyster in the middle of painting. Instead of painting dignified portraits for royalty like Sofonisba (opposite) did, Judith liked to paint regular people relaxing and being happy. Many of her paintings show musicians playing instruments or children having fun. What clues do you see here that show she liked to paint people enjoying themselves?

made around 1630

LOOK CLOSELY

COMPARE AND CONTRAST

Compare the musician's arms and musical instrument with Judith's arms and her tools. Next, compare Judith with Sofonisba. Both women were proud of their role as artists. Look at their outfits, facial expressions, and paintings. What similarities and differences can you find?

OLD-TIME FASHION
The large white circle around the artist's neck is called a ruff. It was a fashionable accessory during the 1600s.

George Bellows, *Lady Jean*

Jean, the artist's daughter, was nine years old when she posed for this portrait. It was a hot summer day in a stuffy room. Her father, American artist George Bellows, wanted to experiment with different colors, shapes, and **patterns** and match her clothing and accessories to the objects in the room. He asked Jean to put on an old-fashioned dress, fancy gloves, and a lacy headscarf. Can you see any ways that Jean managed to express how she felt in this situation?

TRY IT OUT

MAKE BELIEVE

Try copying Jean's pose and facial expression. What words would you use to describe how she looks or feels? What might be making her feel that way?

GETTING PAID
Since Jean did such a good job of modeling, her father paid her the same amount of money that he usually gave to professional grown-up models.

made around 1924

"Smiling" Figure

Just like Jean (opposite), the person in this Mesoamerican sculpture is all dressed up. Their cap and skirt have a lot of **geometric** patterns. The person could be male or female and they are wearing lots of jewelry: a necklace, bracelets, and earrings. They have their mouth open and are holding a gourd rattle in one hand and lifting up their other arm in an energetic way. It looks like they're singing, dancing, and making music.

made in the seventh to eighth century CE

THINK ABOUT

FEELINGS AND EMOTIONS

Both this person and Jean are dressed up in fancy clothes. How are their poses and facial expressions different? What might these clues tell you about how they're feeling?

EXTRA FANCY
Can you spot the small hole in each top corner of this person's cap? Originally, real feathers or tassels may have been tied there, making their outfit even more festive!

Portrait Vessel of a Ruler

This Moche (*MOH-chay*) object from ancient Peru is good at doing two things at once! It's both a portrait of a ruler's head *and* a vessel (a container for holding liquids). Look at the circle-and-stick shape at the top. That's a spout where the liquid comes out *and* a handle for you to grip.

TRY IT OUT

A MATCHING ROBE

In this ruler's community, geometric patterns were used to decorate special clothing and other **textiles** (fabrics). Wearing these patterns meant that you were an important person. Look at the pattern on the ruler's headdress. What shapes do you see? Imagine the ruler is wearing a robe to match the headdress. Try drawing the robe with a similar pattern.

A CONFIDENT LEADER
The lifted head, painted cheeks, and wrinkles between the ruler's brows make him look serious, wise, and confident. What facial expressions and body poses would you make to inspire people to think about you in certain ways?

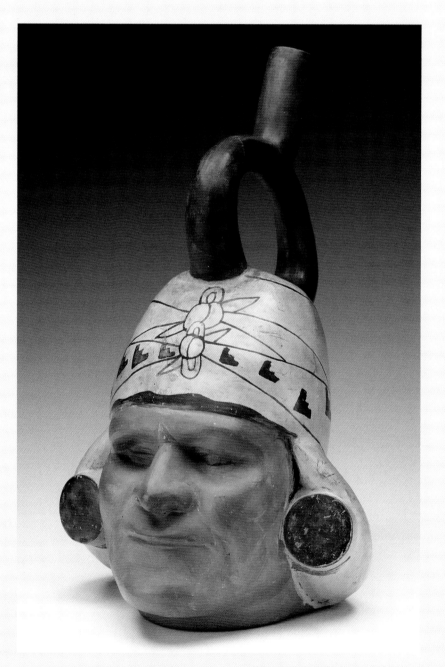

made around 100 BCE–500 CE

Amy Sherald,
He Was Meant for All Things to Meet

Just like the ruler in the vessel (opposite), Keith, the young man in this portrait, has a proud, confident pose. Artist Amy Sherald painted Keith's sweater and the background in a bright lime green. This makes his hair and skin stand out.

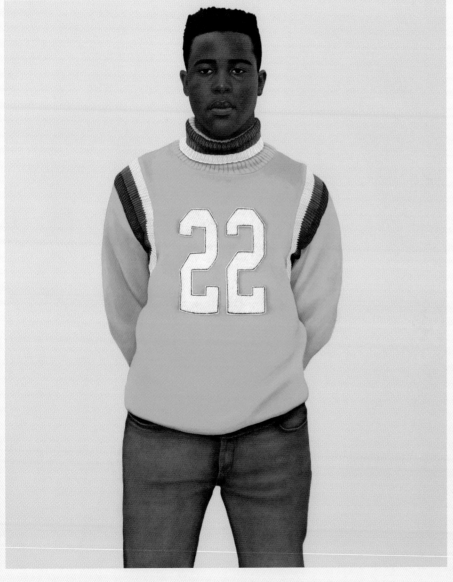

made in 2022

THINK ABOUT

SPORTSWEAR

Keith has on a special sweater that he wears to play lacrosse, a team sport that involves a stick with a net on one end, a ball, and lots of running. How do you feel when you're wearing sports clothes? How do you think Keith feels about his team?

BLACK-AND-WHITE PHOTOGRAPHS

The artist used bright colors everywhere except Keith's skin and hair. For these, she used gray colors to make us think of old-fashioned black-and-white photographs.

Dress Sewn by Rosa Parks

Rosa Parks was an important leader of the civil rights movement in the United States during the 1950s. That means she protested against injustice and fought for equal rights for everybody, especially African Americans. Rosa was also a talented artist. She designed and sewed this dress for a client (customer) who admired her skills.

IMAGINE

A SEASONAL OUTFIT

This dress has a pattern of leaves and flowers printed all over it, which helps the person wearing it think about nature and springtime. Imagine you are designing an outfit for your favorite weather or season. What pattern would you pick so that the wearer would think about the weather or season you chose?

FEEL-GOOD FABRIC
This dress is made from a thin, smooth fabric called viscose. It feels cool and soft on the skin. It has a wrap-style top and a skirt that swirls out wide when you spin.

made in 1955–56

Coty L'Aimant

You can express yourself by choosing not only your clothing, hairstyle, and makeup, but also your scent! Wearing and displaying perfume can be a creative form of self-expression. Coty L'Aimant was a popular perfume in the 1920s, not only because people liked the way it smelled but also because the bottle looked elegant when it was displayed in a bathroom or on a dresser. Three artists teamed up to create it: perfumer Vincent Roubert composed the scent, glassmaker Pierre Camin designed the bottle, and jeweler René Lalique designed the silver stopper (plug).

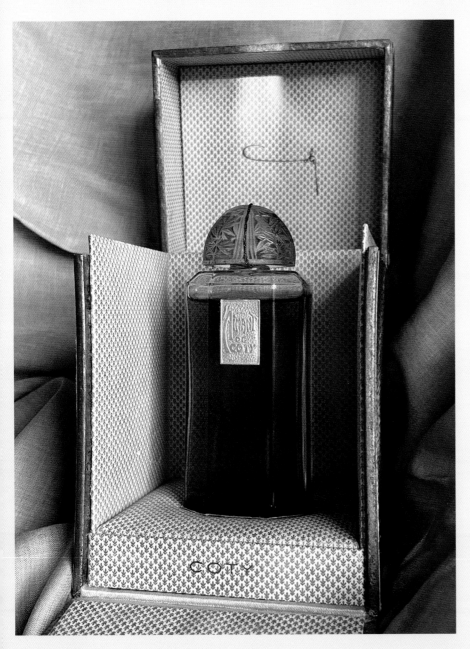

made in 1927

TRY IT OUT

TEAMWORK

Three different types of artists worked together to create L'Aimant. Get together with two other people and collaborate on creating an imaginative perfume by sketching out the bottle design and describing the scent.

WHAT DOES IT SMELL LIKE?
L'Aimant smells like fruits, flowers, and wood. Why might someone want to smell like these things? How might the fragrance affect how they feel?

Locket with Photogr[...]
Harriette and Harry [...]

This locket belonged to Harriette Moore, the [...]
appears in the bottom frame. A photograph of [...]
appears in the top frame. The couple lived in [...]
of the 1900s. They were civil rights activists w[...]
of Florida sign up to vote. The tiny loops at th[...]
Harriette wore it on a chain around her neck[...]
around) reminder of the love she share[...]

TRY IT OUT

IMAGINE THE PATTERN

The top lid of the locket was etched with a decorative floral pattern. Sketch what you think it might look like!

WHO TO CHOOSE
If you had a locket, whose photos would you put inside and why? What do your choices say about your relationship to them?

made around the early to mid-twentieth century

Pair of Ear Ornaments with Winged Runners

These Moche ear ornaments show two runners. Their bodies are a combination of human and bird. Can you spot which parts are human and which are bird? The runners are wearing lots of accessories—headdresses, skirts, bracelets, and boots. They are carrying bags because they are messengers making important deliveries. The wearer could have been a man or a woman, but they would have been of a high status in their society.

made around 400–700 CE

 TRY IT OUT

YOUR OWN DESIGN

Create your own ear ornaments by drawing two circles on paper and filling in a design. Why did you choose this design? What do your choices say about you?

PUZZLE PIECES
The artist arranged tiny pieces of colorful stones and shells next to each other to form the image of the runners. It's like putting together a tiny puzzle or **mosaic**.

Guanyin of the Southern Sea

This painted wood sculpture from China shows a Buddhist holy person named Guanyin. Guanyin's role is to help people in need. Their nickname is "One Who Hears the Cries of the World." They can switch between male and female, or be both. It depends on which is most helpful to the person asking for Guanyin's assistance. In art, Guanyin often wears beautiful robes, scarves, hairdos, and jewelry.

TRY IT OUT

STRIKE A POSE

Guanyin is in a pose called "royal ease." That means both relaxed and dignified. Pretend you are Guanyin. Try copying the position of their arms and legs. How does this pose make you feel? Think about different poses you can make. How does each pose make you feel?

MAGIC MOUNTAIN
The rock that Guanyin is sitting on symbolizes Mount Potalaka, the paradise island where Guanyin lives.

made around 900–1240 CE

Mickalene Thomas,
Portrait of Mnonja

The name of the woman in this modern portrait is Mnonja (*NAHN-jah*). Just like Guanyin (opposite), Mnonja is in a relaxed and dignified pose. She chose her outfit, jewelry, and makeup carefully for this portrait. Mnonja is lying on a couch in a room decorated with lots of colors and patterns. There are patterns with stripes, dots, and flowers. What do these patterns say about Mnonja?

made in 2010

THINK ABOUT

YOUR SELF-PORTRAIT

Imagine you are posing for a portrait. What clothes, accessories, or gestures would you choose to express who you are? What kind of setting would you want to be in? What do these decisions say about you?

EXTRA SPARKLY
Mickalene Thomas likes to add colorful rhinestones (imitation gems) to her paintings to make them sparkle. Can you find all the areas in this portrait where the artist added rhinestones?

CHAPTER 2

HOME AND FAMILY

A family can be people who live together
in the same house or people who live
far apart, in different towns or even on
different continents. You might be related
or you might call yourself family because
of a strong feeling of closeness. No matter
how they look, families often want pictures
that show they belong to each other.
Family portraits and home furnishings
can tell you a lot about the things that are
important to the people in a family.

FAMILY PORTRAITS

Art that shows a family together helps everyone in it feel close, even if some relatives don't live in the same house or see each other every day. Today, most families have photographs that show them together on vacation or at a special occasion. Do you have a favorite family portrait? How does it make you feel?

A FAMILY PORTRAIT IN STONE

Artists have been recording family moments in art since long before cameras were invented. The picture carved on this stone shows a royal family from ancient Egyptian times: the pharaoh Akhenaten, his wife Nefertiti, and three of their daughters. Do you notice how tiny the daughters are? In ancient Egyptian art, artists sometimes made children's bodies look just like grownup bodies, but much smaller, like dolls!

This stone was used as an altar or holy object in a home. At the top, the circle with rays coming out is a symbol, or sign, of the sun god Aten. The pharaoh believed that Aten protected and blessed him and his family.

ANCIENT EGYPTIAN WRITING

In ancient Egyptian art, pictures often appeared along with a type of writing called **hieroglyphs**, made of symbols or small pictures. Here, the hieroglyphs are in rows around the family. They say flattering things about Akhenaten as a pharaoh and ruler. If you could write notes about each person in your family portrait, what would you say?

Notice the faces and bodies of the royal family. Can you find clues that show that they love each other and enjoy spending time together?

Look at the furniture and setting around the family. Do you think the family is indoors in a room or outdoors in nature? What makes you think that?

House Altar Showing Akhenaten, Nefertiti, and Three of Their Daughters, made around 1350 BCE (limestone)

Portrait of the Situ Family

This portrait is of a farming family from rural China. The photo was taken just before Joe (standing on the far left), the eldest son, was sent alone to the United States to earn a better living. He was just nine years old! In his new home in New York City, Joe was raised by an aunt and uncle. He would not get to see his parents and siblings again until thirty years later, when the rest of the family immigrated to join him.

TRY IT OUT

CREATING TOGETHERNESS

Imagine that the Situ family took another group photo the next year. How might they add Joe into the portrait, even though he was far away? Think about a family event that some of your relatives couldn't attend. Using photocopies or printouts of family photos, make a collage that adds them back in.

REUNITING
Joe's mother gave birth to three more siblings after Joe left. He didn't get to meet them until all the siblings reunited as grown-ups.

made in 1955

Kehinde Wiley, *Portrait of Asia-Imani, Gabriella-Esnae, and Kaya Palmer*

This painting shows a modern British family from London. The mother shows her love by holding the hand of the younger daughter while resting her other hand on her older daughter's shoulder. The background was inspired by an 1890s wallpaper designed by British artist William Morris. American artist Kehinde Wiley painted the yellow flowers to weave around the family, showing their connection to each other.

made in 2020

LOOK CLOSELY

STUDIO DÉCOR

Both this portrait and the one of the Situ family were made in artists' studios. What decoration do they share in common? What other similarities can you find between the two portraits?

SIZE MATTERS
The Situ family photograph is small enough to hold in your hands. The painting on this page takes up a whole wall!

Florine Stettheimer,
Family Portrait, II

Artist Florine Stettheimer liked to combine the imaginary with the real in her art. In this family portrait, she's having a party with her mother and sisters in their New York City apartment. There are famous real-life buildings in the background. The three enormous flowers floating in the middle and the view of the ocean in the background are imaginary. Why do you think the artist added these imaginary details? What do they tell you about how she thought about herself and her family?

made in 1933

 # LOOK CLOSELY

HIDDEN ITEMS

Florine wrote her name twice in this painting, along with her sisters' names, Ettie and Carrie. A dragon with a crown, which was a decorative sculpture in Florine's building, is also hiding. Can you find the names and the dragon?

A LOOPY FRAME
The artist also designed the frame for this portrait. It's made of loops, just like the loopy design in the black lace outfits.

James Van Der Zee, *Wedding Day, Harlem*

This photograph also combines the imaginary with the real. The bride and groom are in a photo studio in Harlem, New York City. The chair, carpet, and framed mirror are real, but the fireplace is a painted picture on the wall. Do you notice that the little girl cradling the doll on the carpet is see-through? This means that she's imaginary. What do these details tell you about the hopes the couple may have for the future?

made in 1926

TRY IT OUT

REAL AND IMAGINARY

Use pencils, crayons, or stickers to add imaginary things to copies of your favorite family portrait. How do these change the mood or story of the portrait?

PHOTOGRAPHIC MAGIC
Photographer James Van Der Zee used a special technique to add the little girl's image from another photograph.

HOME ACTIVITIES

Home can be a real place like a building or a house, which gives you protection and shelter from the outside. Home can also describe the feeling of belonging you get when you are around people you love and in a place where you feel comfortable. A lot of important activities can take place inside a home, such as sleeping, eating, and playing. Who are the people you think about when you hear the word "home"? What activities do you do there?

HOUSE PARTY

What does it look like when you have a party at home? In this Mesoamerican sculpture, people are having a party at their house.

To make this sculpture, the artist first shaped clay into a two-story house with two gabled (triangular) roofs. Then they molded smaller pieces of clay into people and placed them throughout the house. The entire sculpture was then heated up in a kiln to harden all the clay and make the sculpture long-lasting.

DIAMOND PATTERN

The house was also originally painted with a black-and-white diamond pattern on the roof and walls. Most of the paint has worn off over time, but you can still see some traces of black.

People are doing so many different things at this party! Can you see someone eating? People having a conversation? Can you spot a person on a balcony playing a musical instrument? How about a person looking out of the window? Can you find people who are relaxing outside? What about someone napping? There are even pets! Can you find all these details?

House Model, made around 100 BCE–200 CE (ceramic)

Sleeping Lady

This clay figurine reminds us about the importance of sleep. It was made during prehistoric times in what is today a country called Malta. The sculpture shows that at the time, bedframes may have been constructed of four beams held up by two pedestals (bases or supports) and mattresses were made of bundled-up straw. Even that long ago, people wanted comfortable places to sleep!

made around 3100 BCE

THINK ABOUT

SLEEPING BEAUTY

The curving outlines of the sleeping woman's arms, hips, and legs create a flow in the way our eyes move. The tassels, dots, and geometric patterns on the dress make the ordinary activity of sleeping seem artful and beautiful.

ART ON A PEDESTAL
As well as providing a place to sleep, the bed functions as a built-in pedestal to show off the woman's body like a work of art.

Mary Cassatt,
Little Girl in a Blue Armchair

American artist Mary Cassatt didn't want to paint the little girl being prim and proper in front of a grown-up audience. Instead, she wanted to show her behaving just as anyone would when they are tired. She is sprawled out in an armchair, ready to fall asleep like her dog. This painting makes us think about how safe, cozy, and peaceful it feels to relax at home.

made in 1878

IMAGINE

BEFORE AND AFTER

The girl is wearing a nice white dress and fancy shoes, with a shawl, hair ribbons, and socks that match each other. It looks like she was dressed for an important occasion. What event do you think she had been to? Think about a "before" image to pair with this "after" picture.

LOOSE BRUSHSTROKES
Do you notice that the paint marks in the flower pattern on the chairs are loose and swirly? This gives the painting a relaxed feeling.

Pierre Bonnard, *The Yellow Shawl*

French artist Pierre Bonnard shows that our home life can inspire art. We can lay out food or flowers in pleasing arrangements. Here, Pierre has tilted the table so that we can see the food and utensils arranged on top. We can decorate our surroundings with textiles in interesting colors and patterns, as shown in the tablecloth, windows, and clothes here. We can artfully plan a meal to share. Notice how the empty chair makes you feel invited to join!

TRY IT OUT

FAMILY FOOD PORTRAIT

Draw a "portrait" of your family's favorite foods laid out on the dining table. What does this tell others about your family?

DECORATING THE HOME
Pierre also designed furniture, fabric patterns, and posters for the home.

made around 1925

Wada Sanzo, Title Unknown
(Four Children Playing a Game)

Japanese artist Wada Sanzo was a costume designer who made clothing for theater performers. That's why there are so many different patterned textiles in this drawing. The children's clothing and the mat they're playing on have interesting colors and fun patterns. Choosing textiles for our home is one way we can be artistic in our daily lives, and this can affect how we feel inside.

made in the first half of the twentieth century

THINK ABOUT

FLOOR GAMES

The children in this drawing are playing a tossing game on the floor. The three books on the mat also show that they've been reading. What kinds of activities do you like doing on the rug or floor? Does doing these activities there feel different than doing them at a table or desk?

SPECIAL TOOL
The large wooden structure in the background on the right is a **loom**. This is a tool used to weave yarn or thread into fabric.

HOME FURNISHINGS

It's not just people that make a home. Furniture, tools, and decorations also play important roles! Home furnishings are the things that make a home useful, comfortable, and fun. Furniture such as beds, chairs, and shelves give us places to sleep, sit, and store our belongings. Vessels such as cups, plates, and bowls help us to eat, drink, and share food. Fabric items such as blankets, rugs, and curtains keep us warm and provide our house with colorful decoration. Photographs, posters, and plants make the walls and rooms more cheerful. Furnishings make your home a place you want to spend time in.

POTS AND PANS

What kinds of pots, pans, and dishes did people use in their kitchens 200 years ago? This toy kitchen was made in Germany or the United States in the 1800s. It can give us a good idea of how kitchens worked back then! All the miniature items are made of wood, metal, or ceramic, just like the full-size versions. Toy sets like this were made to help children learn how to use different tools for performing grown-up tasks. While children did have fun playing with the miniature tools, they also had to be serious about learning how to use each one correctly. These toy sets were supposed to prepare kids to be responsible adults.

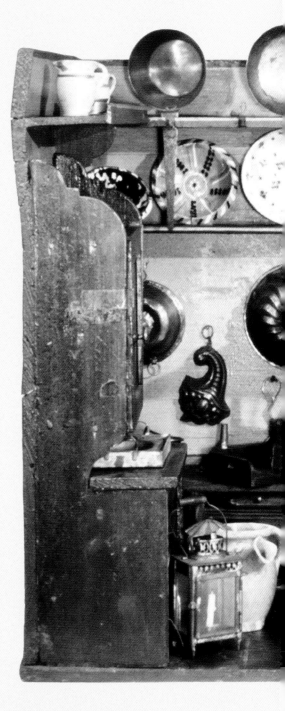

Toy Kitchen,

made around 1830–80
(wood, metal, ceramic)

Do you recognize any of the tools in this kitchen? Choose two of them and pretend you are using them. How would you hold the tool? What task would you perform with it? Do you use it to clean, cook, or prepare something? Now choose two tools that you've never seen before. Look closely at each one. Based on how it looks, can you guess how it was used?

Parein Biscuit Tin

Decorative cookie tins were invented in the 1800s in England. The tins were molded into interesting shapes and printed with fun designs. They were common works of art that people wanted to display in their homes. Parein Biscuits, a Belgian cookie company, sold this tin that's shaped like a house. The inhabitants are welcoming visitors into the house, relaxing in the sun, and enjoying the view from the balcony.

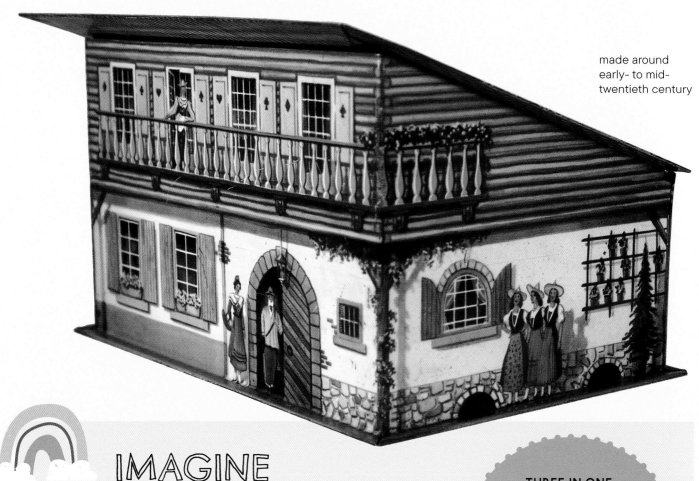

made around early- to mid-twentieth century

IMAGINE

SECRET STORAGE

In the past, people reused cookie tins for storing lots of different things, such as money, crayons, or sewing supplies. What would you keep in this tin?

THREE IN ONE
This object plays many roles: it can store cookies, be displayed as a decoration, or be reused as a storage container. And for the people in this scene, it's a home!

Doña Rosa Solís y Menéndez, Embroidered Coverlet (Colcha)

This blanket was made by a woman named Rosa in Central America in the 1700s. She **embroidered** (sewed) beautiful designs onto it to celebrate her marriage to a man named Gabriel Milanés. The blanket was not only useful for keeping the couple warm, it was also a colorful decoration for the top of their bed. The woman and man at the center are a portrait of Rosa and Gabriel. Their clothes give you an idea of how people dressed back then!

made in 1786

LOOK CLOSELY

NAME SEARCH

The woman sewed her name, Doña Rosa Solís y Menéndez, onto the blanket. Can you spot where she stitched it?

MARRIAGE SYMBOL

The flowering vines are growing on trellises (vertical supports). They symbolize the couple's hope that their marriage will grow to be strong, lush, and beautiful, just like the vines.

Worktable

Do you have a desk where you play, draw, and do your schoolwork? Does it have shelves, cubbies, or drawers for you to store your pencils, crayons, and other tools? This worktable from the 1800s in the United States does the same thing! It was a desk where a person could do crafts like sewing, painting, basket weaving, and crocheting (making clothes and household items with yarn). Back then, worktables were usually used by girls and women.

THINK ABOUT

MOVING AROUND

This worktable can be moved around so that you can craft in different spaces. What clues tell you that the table got moved around a lot?

made around 1805–15

SECRET STASH
This worktable has many hidden shelves, secret drawers, and cubbyholes. What would you keep in these hiding places?

Bowl with Children in a Garden

This bowl was made in China in the 1600s in a city called Jingdezhen, which has been world-famous for over 1,000 years for its **porcelain** dishes and vases. Porcelain is a hard white material made by heating up a fine white clay mineral called **kaolinite**. This porcelain bowl shows a scene of children playing in a garden. The bowl is not only useful for holding food, it's also fun to turn in your hands because the picture goes all the way around!

made around mid-sixteenth century

 TRY IT OUT

COMPLETE THE SCENE

Look closely at the picture. What game do you think the children are playing? Imagine what the other side of the bowl shows. Draw it with blue crayons on a piece of white paper to resemble the colors of this bowl.

PORCELAIN CITY
If you visit Jingdezhen today, you will find that artists are still making porcelain dishes and vases, just like they have for over 1,000 years.

Handle Spout Vessel with Relief Depicting a Standing Figure, Holding Farming Tools

This Moche vessel was made by using fingers to shape and pinch soft clay, then heating the clay to make it solid. It was meant to do two things at once: to hold liquids and to be a work of art. On the flat side of the vessel is a sculpture of a person holding a farming tool in one hand and a tall plant in the other. How are these objects connected to the use of this vessel?

TRY IT OUT

DESIGN YOUR OWN

Do you notice that the shape of the vessel makes it look like the person is standing in an arch? On a piece of paper, draw a large arch and design your own decoration for this part of the vessel.

HIGH STATUS
By showing the person wearing fancy clothes and a headdress, which only important members of the community got to wear, the artist tells us that this object was of high status too.

made around 100 BCE–500 CE

Sam Buganski,
Malibu Mug

This mug is all about fun! When artist Sam Buganski began making it, he wanted to feel like a kid again. He shaped the clay with his hands and painted the outside with cheerful colors. The shapes, dribbles, and dots look like they're dancing. The artist wanted the mug to look a bit messy— because being messy is sometimes fun!

made in 2023

THINK ABOUT

SIMILARITIES AND DIFFERENCES

This mug and the Moche vessel (opposite) were made thousands of years apart, but are both used for holding liquids. What other similarities and differences can you think of?

COMPLETE THE SET
If you were to design a plate, bowl, and utensils to match this mug, what would they look like?

CHAPTER 3

COMMUNITY

A community is a group of people who share things in common, like living on the same street or going to the same school. It's the people who work in the stores, libraries, and parks you go to, who take care of you and help you. It can also be a group of people who share cultural traditions or common interests. Who is in your community? Do you belong to more than one?

TEACHING AND LEARNING

Teaching and learning happen all the time in communities! Grown-ups and elders teach young people important skills, knowledge, and art forms that have been around for a long time. These are traditions. They can be cooking recipes, playing sports, or doing crafts. By teaching and learning together, we make sure that the knowledge and activities can continue in the future. What do you see people teaching and learning in your community?

HONORING A GREAT MUSICIAN

Artist Romare Bearden was born in the American South. When he was a child, he and his family moved to a city in the north called Pittsburgh, Pennsylvania. That was an important memory from his childhood. When Romare made this picture, he wanted to honor jazz musician Mary Lou Williams, who was also born in the American South and moved to Pittsburgh as a child. Romare shows the piano teacher looking over the student's shoulder as she practices piano. By showing Mary Lou this way, Romare is saying that she's an important person in the community. He's also showing that learning and teaching are important for the community.

CREATING A LITHOGRAPH

This artwork is not a painting or collage. It's a **lithograph**. To create this, the artist first uses a greasy crayon to draw a picture on a flat stone. Next, they apply chemicals that make parts of the stone attract or repel greasy ink. Then, they apply the ink to the stone and press a sheet of paper over the ink. The picture then appears on the paper! This method allows the artist to make many prints of the image.

Can you point out all the different kinds of furniture and decoration in this artwork? What does each one add to the atmosphere of the home?

Romare Bearden, *The Piano Lesson,* made in 1984 (lithograph)

Seated Adult and Youth

In many communities, people share wisdom (knowledge about how to live well) by spending time with members of other age groups. This Mesoamerican clay sculpture shows an elder and youth sitting cross-legged on the ground. Their body language tells you that they're enjoying their conversation. The boy leans in and the grown-up rests his arm on the boy's shoulder. Both have lively expressions on their faces.

made around 1050 BCE

IMAGINE

SPEECH BUBBLES

Imagine that there are speech bubbles near the elder's and young person's heads. Fill them in with what you think each person is saying. What is being learned or taught?

SMALL DETAILS
Notice the separate strands of hair. The artist used a sharp tool to scratch thin lines in the clay to create these details.

Henry Ossawa Tanner,
The Banjo Lesson

Just like the sculpture (opposite), this painting shows an older person spending time with a younger person, allowing the knowledge of their community to be passed down to the next generation. American artist Henry Ossawa Tanner made this painting in the 1800s. It shows a grandfather teaching his grandson how to play the banjo. You can tell that this artistic tradition is important to them because they've set aside all other chores to focus on the music lesson.

made in 1893

LOOK CLOSELY

BODY LANGUAGE

Look closely at the grandfather's and grandson's hands and legs. What clues show that the grandfather is supporting the grandson as he plays the banjo? Do you have a skill that you've learned from an older person? How do they show they're supporting you as you learn?

LOOSE BRUSHSTROKES
Notice how loose and blurry the brushstrokes are, especially in the framed pictures on the wall. This makes the painting seem like a memory from the past.

Martha Perkins, Sampler

This sampler was made by a twelve-year-old girl named Martha Perkins in 1773. She lived in Connecticut, North America. In many New England communities at the time, samplers were pieces of cloth that showed off the embroidery (decorative sewing) skills that a girl had learned at home or at school. It displayed her potential to be a useful member of her community. This sampler shows that Martha could embroider numbers, letters, trees, buildings, and people. She was especially good at stitching flowers.

made in 1773

 LOOK CLOSELY

PERSONALIZATION

Can you spot two sheep in Martha's design? Can you also find her name and the year? What does adding her name to this sampler tell you about how Martha felt about her sewing skills?

MANY KINDS OF KNOWLEDGE
By embroidering sentences and numbers, a girl showed that she could read and do math. A sampler showed she would make a good wife, mother, and homemaker—roles that Martha's community valued at this time.

Headdress
(Chi Wara)

This carved wooden sculpture is a chi wara headdress that was made in Mali, West Africa, during the 1900s. Chi wara headdresses show a mythical creature that combines parts of an antelope and an anteater. They were worn by male performers at weddings and agricultural (farming) festivals. Joined by women singing, the performer told the story of how this mythical creature first taught people in the community how to farm.

made around early to mid-1900s

THINK ABOUT

FARMING TOOLS

Can you point out parts of the chi wara's face and body that remind you of farming or gardening tools that people use for digging, raking, or shoveling soil? Why might the chi wara have these?

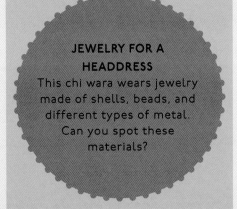

JEWELRY FOR A HEADDRESS
This chi wara wears jewelry made of shells, beads, and different types of metal. Can you spot these materials?

Nizami, *Laila and Majnun* in School

This Persian illustration made in the 1500s in what is now Iran comes from a **manuscript** (book) that tells the love story of two young people, Laila and Majnun. This scene is from when they first met at school. The artist gives us super vision: we see the scene from high up, even through the walls. Everyone is there to learn, play, and practice getting along. It's a place where grown-ups teach children skills that will help the community thrive in the future.

THINK ABOUT

SEARCH AND FIND

Look carefully at the different areas of the school. Can you find Laila and Majnun? What clues tell you that it's them?

DECORATIONS EVERYWHERE
Gold is used to reflect light and make the picture glow. **Calligraphy** is used as wall patterns. Can you find these decorations?

made around 1525 CE

Starfield Library, Seoul

In many communities, schools are not the only places for teaching and learning—public libraries are important too. People don't just visit libraries to read on their own; they gather there to watch performances, hear authors read to an audience, or do group activities such as arts and crafts. Many libraries also feature murals, sculptures, and other kinds of art. Starfield Library in Seoul displays its books in giant wraparound shelves that look like towers. Sometimes the books are arranged to create enormous pictures.

opened in 2017

THINK ABOUT

NATURE IN THE LIBRARY

Even though it's an indoor space, this airy, two-story library features a lot of wood and natural light. How might these natural elements be helpful in a place of reading and learning?

SURPRISING SPOT
The library is built inside a crowded shopping mall in a busy part of the city. How might having a library in this location be useful?

Faith Ringgold,
Dancing at the Louvre

In many communities, quilts are made by groups of people, each of whom contributes pieces and images reflecting their values. Artist Faith Ringgold uses quilting to honor this tradition in Black communities. In the 1990s, she made twelve quilts that tell of an African American woman named Willia who moves from New York City to Paris. Here, she shows how grown-ups pass down their love of art to children. The quilt shows Willia dancing in an art museum with her friend Marcia and Marcia's three daughters.

LOOK CLOSELY

MIXED MEDIA

When artists use many types of materials and techniques in an artwork, it's called **mixed media**. The artist used words and pictures to tell Willia's story, combining ink, fabric, and paint. Can you see where she used each type of material?

made in 1991

ART INSIDE ART
Hanging on the wall are three paintings by Italian artist Leonardo da Vinci. Find pictures of these paintings online or in a book and compare them to how they look here.

Raphael Soyer, *Dancing Lesson*

A family can be a type of community, especially when cultural skills are encouraged. In this 1920s painting, Raphael Soyer shows his sister Rebecca teaching Raphael's twin brother, Moses, to dance. Behind them, Israel, the youngest sibling, accompanies them on the harmonica. Their mother and father watch from the couch, drawing them into the collective effort. The only person not interested is the grandmother, who's asleep!

made in 1926

TRY IT OUT

FIND THE PORTRAITS

The black-and-white portrait is of the artist's grandparents. In this book, can you find three other family portraits?

FAMILY AND CULTURE

Raphael's Jewish family immigrated to the US from Russia in the early 1900s. The newspaper held by the artist's mother uses the Hebrew alphabet and Yiddish words, the language the family spoke at home.

BEING TOGETHER

Communities go through a lot together. When something sad or unexpected happens, a community can come together to mourn or support each other. When people face problems, a community might gather to find solutions. For most people, the best part of being in a community is celebrating and having fun together! Communities might do this by having parties, playing games, or sharing a meal.

PART OF A SHELF

Artist Zizwezenyanga Qwabe made this wood carving in KwaZulu-Natal in South Africa between the 1920s and 1950s. It is a panel that is meant to be used as part of a storage shelf. Can you spot the four small holes in the corners? Those are places for nails or pegs to be inserted to attach the panel to the shelf.

Zizwezenyanga Qwabe, *Storage-Rack Panel,*

made around late 1920s–40s (boxwood)

A VILLAGE SCENE

The artist used the panel's rectangular shape to carve a village scene filled with people, animals, and houses. On the left is a row of women carrying jars and vessels of food and water on their heads. In the middle is a group of houses and a circular fence filled with cattle. On the right, a group of men meet with the community leader. What do you see that tells you they are meeting to make an important decision that affects the whole village? What activities are groups performing to contribute to this event?

In this carving, some of the people's bodies are facing the front, in a **frontal position**. Others are facing the side, in **profile**. Take a close look at the people in this carving. Can you point out who's in a frontal position and who's in profile?

Bayeux Tapestry

This picture shows a scene from an epic tale about two men named William and Harold battling each other with their armies to win the throne of a kingdom. It was sewn onto a long roll of fabric with a needle and yarn. Here, the men in William's army enjoy a meal together as a community. Even though being in an army is difficult, spending time together might help the men work better as a team.

made around 1075

IMAGINE

ON A ROLL

This French artwork is almost 900 years old! Imagine a story told in pictures on a roll of toilet paper. Instead of turning pages, you unroll the sheets to find out how the story goes. That's how the Bayeux Tapestry works!

WORDS ON CLOTH
William and Harold's story is told mostly in lots of pictures, helped by some words in Latin.

Maharana Jagat Singh Attending the Raslila

In this 1700s picture made in India, attributed to the painter Jai Ram and/or Jiva, we see people in a palace courtyard celebrating the festival of Diwali. The party takes place under the moonlight. The king and a group of musicians are sitting on the left side. Opposite, a group of dancers perform a story of Krishna, a Hindu god. People are doing different things to contribute to the event. What roles are they playing?

made in 1736

IMAGINE

OTHER SOUNDS

There must be a lot of music inside the courtyard. What might it sound like in other areas of the palace? Is it quieter? Are there any other sounds?

BIRD'S-EYE VIEW
The artist has painted this scene from a **bird's-eye view** so we are like a bird flying in the air, looking down. How does this make you more aware of the different roles?

Model of a Ballgame with Spectators

In this Mesoamerican clay sculpture, people have gathered around a court to watch players compete in a ball game. The audience have their arms around each other as they cheer for their team. Some have blankets wrapped around their bodies to keep warm. A few people are walking up the stairs—maybe they're late to the game!

IMAGINE

TEAM COLORS

This clay sculpture was originally painted. Which colors would you use for each team's outfits? How do shared colors help team members feel closer to one another?

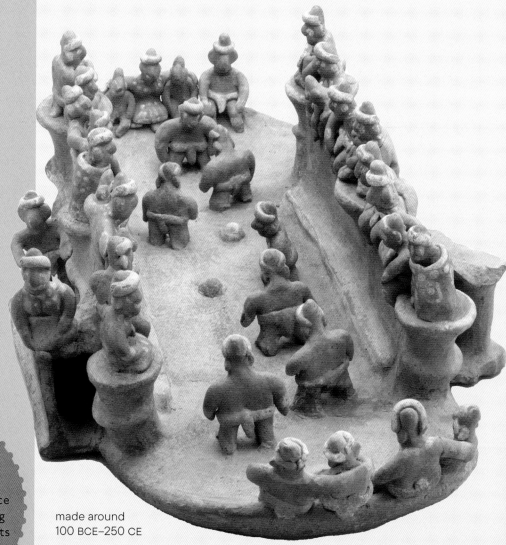

made around
100 BCE–250 CE

COMMUNITY EXPRESSION
Community members bond at sports games by sharing wins and losses. This audience shows this bond by huddling together. In community events you've gone to, how do people express their closeness?

Panel from a Casket with Scenes from Courtly Romances

This ivory carving made in France in the 1300s shows us some important activities from the royal court, the community that formed around the king and queen during the medieval period in Europe. In the central scene, there are two knights in armor, charging at each other on horseback. The sharp ends of their lances have been made less pointy so they don't hurt each other in this friendly game. In the balcony above, people have gathered to watch.

made around 1330–50

THINK ABOUT

GAMES AND COMPETITIONS

Both this carving and the sculpture (opposite) show games and competitions. How can cheering or playing for the same team help people bond? How can competing for fun be positive for the community?

COURTLY LOVE
The side scenes show knights pursuing love in the court. During the medieval period in Europe, courtly love was a set of behaviors that unmarried couples followed. What rules do your communities have?

Funerary Relief of a Vegetable Vendor

This terra-cotta sculpture was made in Italy almost 1,000 years ago! It shows a woman selling vegetables at her food stand. Notice the produce laid out across the counter and the baskets piled around her. The fact that someone made an artwork showing this vegetable vendor tells us she was an important community member. Who in your community do you think deserves to have art made about them?

TRY IT OUT

WORKING AT A STORE

What would you sell at your own store that would be wanted by the people in your community, and why? Draw a shop counter and include any items you would sell.

SLANTED PERSPECTIVE
The artist made the counter tilt toward you so you can see the items on it. Where else in this book does an artist tilt the table to show everything on top?

made around 150–200 CE

John Heywood, Miss Harrison's Sweet Shop: House of Nectar

This photograph was taken in Boston, Massachusetts, in the 1980s. It shows a candy store filled from floor to ceiling with sweets. The storekeeper has a huge smile on her face as she collects money from a young customer. One girl is looking down—maybe she's having a hard time deciding which candy bar to buy?

made in 1989

THINK ABOUT

COMPARE THE ROLES

This photograph and the terra-cotta sculpture (opposite) were made almost 900 years apart, but both show women shopkeepers selling goods. The shopkeeper role has been important for a long time. What other similarities and differences can you find?

CANDY TIME
The clock hands show it is almost two o'clock. It must be Saturday or Sunday, as in the US, children are usually in school until three o'clock on weekdays.

CHAPTER 4

SOCIETY

A society is a large population of people that represents many different communities. It includes groups who might speak different languages, belong to different cultural identities, or have different ways of living. What they share in common is a way of being organized so that everyone can be safe and have what they need. Everyone in a society should share equal rights, laws, and resources like water, food, and shelter.

MANY COMMUNITIES, ONE SOCIETY

A society is similar to a community, but much bigger. You usually don't get to meet every person in a society! Most of us belong to small, close-knit communities whose members we are familiar with. But when we go out to public spaces like streets, parks, and big events, we come in contact with other members of society who might belong to other communities. Even though we may come from different backgrounds, we try to get along so everyone's common needs are met. That's how a society is supposed to work!

SHARED RESOURCES

In this painting, Ralph Fasanella shows people riding the subway in New York City. (In other cities, this type of public transit system might be called the metro or the underground.) Ralph rode the subway every day, and he made this painting based on his sketches of the passengers. Look closely at the riders' facial expressions and postures. What clues tell you they're strangers? Even though they might not know each other, how are they functioning as a society in this moment? What common goals or interests might they share?

SELLING TO SOCIETY

Take a close look at the posters on the walls of the subway car. What services, products, or events are these ads trying to sell? What kinds of things do they believe people in society need or want? What do you think most people need or want?

Each passenger seems to be in their own little world. Imagine there's a thought bubble beside each person's head. What would you write inside?

Some of the passengers are sitting and some are standing. In the public spaces where you've been, who sits and who stands? What might this say about them?

Ralph Fasanella, *Subway Riders,* made in 1950 (oil on canvas)

Gordon Parks, *Untitled*

Photographer Gordon Parks captures a city scene that shows cooperation among members of society. Even though there are lots of vehicles and crowds on the street, they are respectfully sharing the space. The cars make room for the parade heading down the road, and the marchers move in tidy rows. Even the trees, buildings, and streetlamps are lined up to give the place a feeling of order and direction.

THINK ABOUT

MOVIES AND FASHION

Gordon took photos for fashion magazines and made movies. Can you point out details in this photograph that suggest these other interests?

BLURRED LINES
The blurry diagonal line on the upper left is a telephone wire that was in the camera's way, but the photographer kept the detail in. It matches the direction of the row of trees, adding to the balance and order of the scene.

taken around 1948

Benton Spruance,
The People Work—Evening

Artist Benton Spruance shows that city streets and transit systems are places where members of society often cross paths. Three levels of the city are visible: the street level is filled with cars and buses, the underground level has trains and tunnels, and the elevated railway rises up in the background. People are everywhere! Even so, there's a feeling of cooperation and organization. Can you point out things that help create safety and order in this busy area?

made in 1937

THINK ABOUT

BLACK-AND-WHITE ART

Like Gordon Parks's photograph (opposite), this lithographic print shows a city scene using black-and-white tones. What other similarities and differences can you find between the photograph and the print?

HATS ON
Back in the 1930s, it was common for everyone to wear hats outdoors. Can you spot anyone in this scene *not* wearing a hat?

Benjamin West, *Agrippina Landing at Brundisium with the Ashes of Germanicus*

When something unfortunate happens in a society, people gather to support those who are hurt. American-born Benjamin West painted such an occurrence from ancient Roman history. After Roman general Germanicus dies while overseas, his family brings his ashes home on a ship. As they enter their hometown, people come out to watch and share in the family's grief. How does the family show that they're mourning?

made in 1768

THINK ABOUT

EXPRESSING EMOTIONS

The crowd represents people from many parts of society. Some are young, some are elderly, some wear uniforms that show their profession (job). How are people expressing their sadness?

STILL THE SAME?
When an unfortunate event happens today, do people respond in the same ways as they did back then? Do people in different societies react in similar ways to tragic occurrences? Why?

Bronislaw Bak, *Parade,*
from *One-Hundred Views of Chicago*

Although people in a society might each belong to smaller, close-knit communities, there are usually large societal events that everyone participates in. In this woodblock print by Bronislaw Bak, people from different parts of society gather for a parade. Like the crowd shown opposite, the participants here vary in age and profession, but this time, the mood is different. How would you describe the atmosphere of this occasion?

made in 1967

IMAGINE

SOUNDSCAPES

Imagine you are watching the parade. What sounds do you hear and what feelings go with them? Now imagine you are part of the group gathered around Germanicus's family (opposite). What do you hear and what are your matching emotions?

SURFACE DETAILS
Can you spot details that tell you this was printed from a woodblock? Why might an artist choose one kind of art over another to express their ideas?

Great Mosque of Djenné, Mali

Although not everyone in society belongs to a religious community, religious buildings are often important **landmarks** in a region. The Great Mosque of Djenné (*JEN-NAY*) in Mali is made of mudbrick, which melts over time from rain. Every year, the city gathers to apply fresh mud, sourced from two local rivers, to the enormous structure. Replastering is hard work, but people treat it like a celebration! Musicians provide entertainment, children play, and elders share their memories of this tradition.

built around the thirteenth century

 IMAGINE

WORK AND PLAY

When people replaster the Great Mosque, they turn the work into a festival. Can you think of a major task in your society that needs to be accomplished by a lot of people? How can the work be turned into play?

FUNCTIONAL DECORATION
The sticks poking out of the building form a decorative pattern, but they also support the walls.

Colosseum, Rome

The Colosseum was an ancient Roman building where people watched animal hunts and contests between gladiators (professional fighters). It's one of the largest arenas in the world, with three levels decorated with arches. Inside, the emperor and his officials sat in the front rows; government leaders, nobles, and businesspeople occupied the rows behind them; and working people and women sat at the back. What does the seating system say about this society?

built in 70–80 CE

THINK ABOUT

LANDMARKS

Both the Colosseum and the Great Mosque (opposite) are landmarks (buildings that attract attention due to their size, history, and beauty). What are the landmarks where you live, and what draws people to them?

CROWD CONTROL
Tickets to the Colosseum told people which entrances to use. This helped control the crowds and allowed people to get to their seats quickly. We use this same system in arenas today!

BUILT ENVIRONMENTS

A long time ago, people didn't live in permanent (long-lasting) houses. Instead, they temporarily sheltered in caves and tents in their environments (surroundings). They wandered from place to place, searching for food and water. Later, as people built more permanent dwellings, they clustered together and formed communities. They started to farm and raise animals so they could have food and wool right where they lived. Local resources provided water, wood, and other materials they needed. These communities became villages.

Some communities became large societies, where common rules and interests guided the population on how to cooperate and share resources. These societies constructed towns and cities that included housing, public spaces, and **infrastructure** (roads, bridges, and tunnels). These provided people with shelter and meeting places, methods of transporting people and goods from place to place, and common spaces for recreation and relaxation.

VILLAGES, TOWNS, CITIES

Villages are small communities in the countryside where there are lots of farms and open land. Cities are much bigger and busier, with lots of people, buildings, and public transit systems. Towns are somewhere in between; they have less open space than villages but are much quieter and less crowded than cities. Do you live in a village, town, or city? What kinds of infrastructure does it have?

Panel (from a Settee),

made around 1745–55 (linen)

EMPTY AND FULL

This village scene was sewn onto fabric with silk and wool in England in the 1700s and was used as a sofa cover. Although the village is filled with castles, towers, and gazebos (open-air structures with roofs), it's missing one important thing that would make it a living society: people!

If this scene were filled with people, what are the different roles they would play for the village to run smoothly and look this well-tended?

Shibam, Yemen

Shibam in Yemen is one of the oldest high-rise cities in the world, and it is still inhabited by people today. It was built in the middle of a desert and has around 500 mudbrick buildings that rise between five and eleven stories, casting shadows that shade people from the sun. Since rain, wind, and heat wear away at the walls, everyone in this society gathers regularly to apply new layers of mud to keep the buildings intact.

built in the third century

THINK ABOUT

EXTREME CITY

Imagine this city was built in a tropical rainforest, a snowy mountain range, or another extreme environment. How might the buildings' materials be different? What must society do to maintain the city's condition?

SHADY STORAGE
The coolest places in Shibam are the ground floors of buildings. That's where people store grain and tend to their farm animals.

Machu Picchu, Peru

Machu Picchu was an ancient city built during the 1400s on top of the Andes Mountains in Peru. It was home to the Inca emperor and a society of over 750 farmers, servants, and other workers. Today, the walls of nearly 200 of the city's stone structures are still standing. Terraces (wide, flat steps) were built along the sides of the mountain so that crops could grow there.

built in the fifteenth century

 IMAGINE

PICTURE POSTCARD

Unlike Shibam (opposite), people no longer live in Machu Picchu, but many tourists visit. Imagine you are visiting Machu Picchu and want to send a postcard to a friend. Draw the city on one side and write a message on the back describing your view.

WELL-CONNECTED
Although Machu Picchu was located up in the mountains, many who lived there came from all over Peru. There were lots of roads that connected the surrounding areas to the city.

Yin Xiuzhen, *Portable City: Hangzhou*

Imagine opening up a suitcase and out pops a city! Whenever Chinese artist Yin Xiuzhen (*SHIW-jen*) decides to make a new *Portable City*, she travels to the city and collects clothes from the people who live there. Then, inside a suitcase, she uses the fabric to create a miniature version of the city's buildings, bridges, and other landmarks. The artist constructs each city from memory. She calls them "portable cities" because she can zip them up and take them wherever she goes. She's made over forty so far!

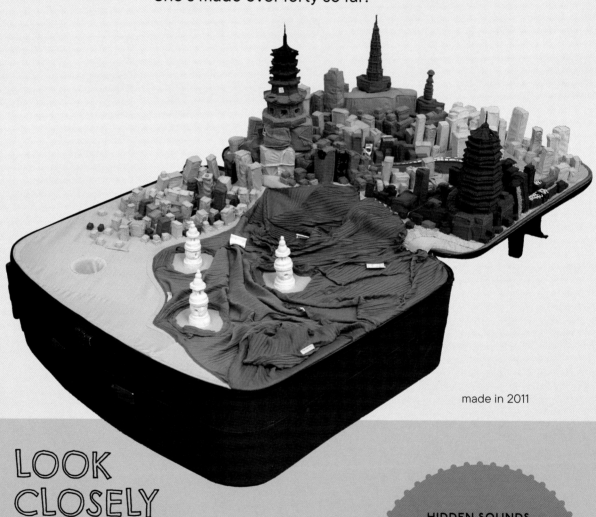

made in 2011

LOOK CLOSELY

CLOTHING INSPECTION

Look closely at the water. The waves are folds and wrinkles from several shirts. The hole on the bottom left is a shirt cuff or collar that imitates a vortex. What other details tell you that the city is constructed from clothing?

HIDDEN SOUNDS
In each suitcase, the artist hides a tape recorder that plays the sounds of the city she visited. What do you think you would hear for this city?

Mohamad Hafez,
Unsettled Nostalgia

American artist Mohamad Hafez spent his childhood in Syria and Saudi Arabia. In this sculpture, he re-creates a street scene from his memories. He uses plaster and found objects like fabric, metal, and wood to make the trees, windows, and laundry hanging from the balconies. Even though there are no people in the sculpture, the numerous doors, windows, and tiny details produce a feeling of the lively society.

made in 2014

THINK ABOUT

HOMESICKNESS

Both this artist and Yin Xiuzhen (opposite) made art to help ease their homesickness. If you are feeling homesick for a place that's special to you, what kind of art can you make to help you feel better?

WALL WRITING
Do you notice the black and red writing on the walls? This is Arabic, a language commonly spoken in the cultures and communities the artist grew up in.

Little Island,
New York City

Cities are crowded places, so public parks are necessary for people to relax, play, and exercise. Little Island, a park in New York City, looks like a forest growing on top of a group of white mushrooms floating on the water. It was constructed from hundreds of tulip-shaped concrete structures. The stems reach down into the river, while the bases support a rolling landscape of winding paths and greenery.

opened in May, 2021

THINK ABOUT

ACCESSIBILITY

Little Island is an accessible space, which means it's friendly to all kinds of people and their needs, including children and the elderly, people who use mobility aids, and people who have visual or hearing impairments. How are places in your society made to be accessible?

SENSE-ATIONAL
Little Island has hundreds of species of plants that attract many kinds of birds and pollinators. The wide variety of vegetation and wildlife is meant to energize and renew people's senses.

Lumphini Park, Bangkok

Lumphini Park was private land that belonged to the king of Siam (now called Thailand), but in 1925 he dedicated it as a public park so that society could enjoy its resources. Aside from trees, lawns, and gardens, there's a public library, numerous playgrounds, and an artificial (human-made) lake for boating. Bangkok's inhabitants treasure this park because it's a rare public space that everyone can use.

built in the 1920s

 TRY IT OUT

A PURPOSEFUL PARK

Although parks may seem natural because they contain rocks and greenery, many were specially designed to serve the needs of society. Draw your own park design and label how different areas fulfill different needs.

A HOLY NAME
Lumphini Park is named after the birthplace of the Buddha, a holy figure. What does this tell you about this figure's status in society?

Jean Tinguely and Niki de Saint Phalle, Stravinsky Fountain

This fountain in Paris, designed by artists Jean Tinguely and Niki de Saint Phalle, features a shallow pool decorated with sixteen sculptures that spin, rotate, and spew water. The sculptures include a mermaid, an elephant, a snake, a skeleton, a hat, and a pair of red lips. The artists wanted the fountain to have a circus atmosphere, and designed the sculptures to match the music of Russian composer Igor Stravinsky.

IMAGINE

MUSIC AND MOVEMENT

Look up videos showing these sculptures in motion and play some of Stravinsky's music. How might spending time by the fountain affect people's moods and actions? What is its role in society?

ARTISTIC PARTNERS
The two artists weren't just partners in designing the fountain—they were also married to each other! Have you ever worked with a family member on a creative project? What was that like for you?

made in 1983

Si-o-se-pol (Allahverdi Khan Bridge), Isfahan

In the Farsi language, *si-o-se-pol* (*see-OH-suh-pohl*) means "bridge of thirty-three arches." That's how many arches decorate this structure overlooking one of the longest rivers in Isfahan, Iran! Si-o-se-pol is both a bridge that spans water and a dam that holds water back. It's also a public space where people meet to take evening walks, play sports, and sit under the arches to chat.

built in the early seventeenth century

THINK ABOUT

WATERWAYS

Clean water keeps us healthy when we drink and bathe in it, but the Stravinsky Fountain and Si-o-se-pol suggest that being near water is helpful to society for other reasons too. What are some of these reasons?

PAINTED BRIDGE
Colorful paintings once covered the walls of Si-o-se-pol. Trace the bridge shape and fill it with your own designs. What kind of atmosphere do your choices create?

Ernest Zacharevic,
Little Children on a Bicycle

Ernest Zacharevic (*zak-uh-RAY-vitch*) painted this street mural in the Malaysian city of Georgetown, Penang. The two children were painted onto the wall, but the bike is a real object that the artist propped against it. Together, they create the illusion that the kids are riding the bike. How might this street look and feel different without the artwork? How does adding public art to walls, buildings, and other outdoor spaces affect how people think of their surroundings?

made in 2012

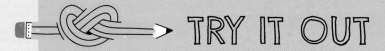 TRY IT OUT

ALTERNATIVE SCENES

Imagine that you took away the bike and added another object to the wall. What new experience does that create for the two kids? Sketch the scene.

ROLE MODELS
Two children from the neighborhood posed for the artist when he created this mural. How might having your image included in public art affect how you feel about yourself and your surroundings?

Elizabeth Catlett, *Students Aspire*

This bronze sculpture by Elizabeth Catlett adorns the School of Engineering at Howard University in Washington, D.C. It shows two students reaching up to cradle a circular disc bearing an equal sign. The other discs show gears, a protractor, and other engineering equipment. The students' feet rest on a tree trunk with visible roots. What do the students' poses and the symbols say about the school's views on education and society?

made in 1977

THINK ABOUT

PUBLIC ART

Think of a public space near you that could benefit from having art added. What would you make to adorn it, and how might your art change people's interactions with that space?

PROUD GRADUATE
The artist attended Howard University as a student. If you could design a public artwork for your school, what would you include to symbolize the school's values?

CHAPTER 5

NATURE

Nature is everything in our world that's not made or caused by humans. It includes living organisms such as plants and creatures; natural energy sources such as sunlight and water; and weather events such as rain, snow, and wind. People have always been fascinated by nature's beauty and power. Throughout history, people have tried to understand, honor, and control nature through science, technology, religion, and art.

ECOSYSTEMS

An ecosystem is like a society, but instead of just humans it includes everything in an environment. It's the interactions of all living and nonliving things in a region, including local weather patterns and land formations. Living things include microorganisms, plants, and creatures, while nonliving things include rocks, soil, water, and sunlight. The health of an ecosystem depends on everything working together in a balanced way. If one part changes, stops working, or becomes extinct, it can throw the rest of the ecosystem off-balance, causing harm to the environment.

LIVING TAPESTRY

A **tapestry** is a textile woven with colorful threads on a loom. Artist Ali Seliem learned to weave when he was a boy at a tapestry school in his village in Egypt. His teachers encouraged him to find inspiration in his surroundings. This tapestry features the landscape, climate, and wildlife of a nearby ecosystem. How do the living and nonliving things interact? How might this tapestry motivate people to care about their ecosystems?

HUMAN ACTIVITY

Throughout history, people's activities have influenced the balance of ecosystems in helpful and harmful ways. When we care for plants and creatures, we can encourage the wellness of our local ecosystems. When we irresponsibly use too much of a resource, we can create pollution or cause imbalances that damage the environment. Since we rely on a healthy planet to live, it's important that we see ourselves as connected to all things that inhabit it. What actions can we take to make our Earth a healthy home for all? How can art help us to do this?

The artist treasures the Ramses Wissa Wassef Art Centre, where he learned to weave. Can you find a detail that tells you this?

Ali Seliem, *Animals by the watering hole,*

made in 1985 (wool, hand-dyed and woven)

Maize God Emerging
from a Flower

In this painted ceramic figurine, the Maize God is adorned with a lavish headdress, ear ornaments, and a necklace. He emerges as a corncob from a husk or a pistil from a water lily—a flower which, in the Maya culture, is connected with the underworld. Hundreds of figurines like this were found at a high-status burial site in Mexico. They might symbolize the Maya people's beliefs about the cycle of birth, death, and renewal. What does this tell us about how the Maya culture viewed the role of humans in the ecosystem?

THINK ABOUT

BURIAL RITUALS

What does the figurine's shape say about how it may have been used in a burial ritual? What do the Maize God's facial expression and posture suggest about his mood?

SECRET WHISTLE
The hollow stem of the figurine produces a whistling sound when air is blown through the figure's head. Why might a work of art also have a practical function?

made around
600–900 CE

Georgia O'Keeffe, *The Lawrence Tree*

Throughout her life, Georgia O'Keeffe found artistic inspiration in flowers, shells, and other natural specimens from her surroundings. She made this painting based on her experience lying on a bench beneath a ponderosa pine tree, gazing up at the night sky. The **worm's-eye view** makes us feel like tiny earthly creatures connected to the vast sky through the dramatic rise of the giant tree. What does this say about how the artist saw the relationship between humans and nature?

made in 1929

 # IMAGINE

COMBINE THE STORIES

Imagine you are in the position of the Maize God in the ceramic figurine (opposite). How might this painting be his perspective of the world?

TURN IT AROUND
Try looking at the painting of the tree upside down. Which perspective do you prefer, and why?

Utagawa Hiroshige, *Sudden Shower over Shin-Ōhashi Bridge and Atake*

This woodblock print by Utagawa Hiroshige depicts a sudden downpour on a bridge spanning Sumida River in central Tokyo. This type of rain occurs late in the day during summer, with the sky suddenly growing dark and releasing thick sheets of rain. In Japanese culture, this is described as "the evening descent of the thunder god." How do this description and the print portray nature's power over human activities?

IMAGINE

RAIN ON WOOD

The artist depicts rain with long, sharp vertical lines. What arm movements do you think he made to carve these? How might the marks convey the sensation of rain against your skin?

ARTISTIC HOMAGE
The Dutch artist Vincent van Gogh admired this print so much that he made a copy using oil paint. Look up his version and compare it to this one.

made in 1857

Emily Kame Kngwarreye, *Earth's Creation*

At 9 feet (2.7 meters) high and 20 feet (6 meters) wide, this painting by Emily Kame Kngwarreye is monumental! To create this landscape of lush, blooming vegetation, Emily laid the canvas flat on the ground and moved her body all around to apply strokes of paint. What do her actions of bending over, kneeling next to, and circling the canvas say about how she views her body's role in art and nature?

made in 1994

THINK ABOUT

BODIES IN NATURE AND ART

Emily was trained as a ceremonial painter in her Aboriginal community in Alhakere, Central Australia. This involved painting designs on women's bodies as a part of awelye, a social and healing ceremony. How do this painting and the print (opposite) involve the body in their creation and effects?

ART ON THE GROUND
Paint a landscape while sitting at a desk and then again while sitting on the floor. How does your body move and feel differently?

Mask

Made of wood, plant fiber, iron nails, and feathers, this Yup'ik mask from Alaska depicts a hunter's kayak. The face of a seal spirit emerges from the center while another animal spirit hovers above. Fish and flippers encircle the boat while a thin rope of wood crowns the top. The tiny beak below the seal spirit's head might depict the hunter as viewed from the prey's perspective. How does this mask present the relationship between hunter and prey within their ecosystem? How might wearing it affect the wearer's feelings toward nature?

IMAGINE

MASKING UP

How would you feel wearing this mask? If you were to design your own version, what objects or symbols would you add? How would wearing it change how you feel and act?

SPECIAL MATERIALS
What do the materials used to make this mask say about the artist's relationship with nature?

made around 1900

Basawan and Dharmdas, *Akbar*

In the late 1500s, the Mughal emperor Akbar commissioned a writer and numerous artists to compose and illustrate a book about his life called the *Akbarnama*. This scene, illustrated by Basawan and Dharmdas, depicts one of Akbar's favorite pastimes: hunting wild animals in the city of Agra. Akbar is the hunter on horseback at the center. Identify all the living and nonliving things in this scene. What role does each play? What does this scene tell you about how Akbar felt about nature?

made around 1590–1595

THINK ABOUT

HUNTER AND PREY

How do this illustration and the mask (opposite) depict hunting? What does each piece of art convey about the roles of hunter and prey in the ecosystem?

WELL-EQUIPPED
The members of the emperor's hunting party use many kinds of equipment for the chase. What purpose do you think each piece of equipment serves?

Grandma Moses,
Grandma Moses Goes to the Big City

Anna Mary Robertson Moses, popularly known as Grandma Moses, found her artistic inspiration in the countryside. The bird's-eye view over this scene allows us to see multiple ecosystems at work, including farmland, orchards, meadows, forests, mountains, and waterways. Tucked in the upper left is a nearby village. Which figure do you think is Grandma Moses, and why might she need to go to the city? What does her trip say about the relationship between the rural countryside and big cities at that time?

made in 1946

 LOOK CLOSELY

ORDERING NATURE

What details tell you that people have worked hard to organize and control parts of the land for different purposes?

A LIFELONG ARTIST
Although Grandma Moses didn't begin painting on canvas until she was seventy-eight years old, she made art her entire life. She sewed quilts, embroidered textiles, and used housepaint to decorate fireplace screens.

Morgain Bailey,
Mississippi Mud

Photographer Morgain Bailey travels across the United States to capture scenes of diverse landscapes and ecosystems. Usually, there are no people in their photos, but they often include traces of human influence. What kinds of human activities have occurred here, and how can you tell? What roles might this field and the forest play in the local ecosystem? What do you think lies beyond the forest?

made in 2023

THINK ABOUT

COMBINE THE PICTURES

Where in Grandma Moses's landscape (opposite) would you slot in this photo, and how would this change your feelings about both landscapes?

BLURRED LINES
Is the blurry line going across the foreground wire fencing or a reflection of a telephone wire? What might the presence of each tell you about the ecosystem?

INSPIRED BY NATURE

Since prehistoric times, humans have been inspired to represent nature in art. The earliest artworks were paintings of animals on cave walls and rock surfaces. Later, people created pottery, sculptures, and textiles that expressed their fear, curiosity, and admiration toward nature's beauty and power. Through art, they explored humans' place and purpose within the natural world.

FEELINGS ABOUT NATURE

Some works of art express the human wish to be in harmony with nature—to feel a part of the sea, sky, earth, and air. Other artworks show people's attempt to understand and learn from nature, like it's a book filled with knowledge and secrets. Artists also make works that express how small and powerless they feel compared to nature's vastness, viewing it with awe and fear, or they use their art to reveal their wishes to own and control nature for their own status or power. How would you express your own feelings about nature through art?

UNDER THE SEA

This ceramic vase looks like it recently washed ashore, with seashells, damp seaweed, and crayfish still clinging to it! Although these natural elements were carefully molded and applied to the vase, Cincinnati potter Thomas Jerome Wheatley wanted the vessel to look like it came directly from nature, with little to no human effort involved in its creation. He may have also wanted to show off how closely he could mimic nature itself! What does the vase's appearance say about how the artist viewed nature and humans' ability to imitate it through art?

To create your own nature-inspired vessel, collect seashells, leaves, or other natural specimens and attach them to a ceramic mug using glue, string, or mesh.

Thomas Jerome Wheatley, Vase

made around 1880–82 (buff earthenware, colored slip, and polychrome and colorless glaze)

Great Serpent Mound, Peebles, Ohio

The Great Serpent Mound is a monumental earthen sculpture constructed by ancient Indigenous peoples in southwestern Ohio, US. It measures 1,300 feet (400 meters) long and 1–3 feet (30–90 centimeters) high. Seen from above, it appears as a giant serpent slithering across the landscape, its outlines following the rise and fall of the land. The oval in the head is thought to represent an enlarged eye, a hollow egg, or the sun.

THINK ABOUT

SUN MARKER

When the sun sets on the longest and shortest days of the year, it lines up perfectly with the serpent's head and tail, respectively. Why do you think people built this monument to match the sun's movement throughout the year?

CONTINUOUS CARE

It's still a mystery who originally created this monument, but some experts believe that several Indigenous groups played a role in designing, building, and maintaining it.

built over 2,000 years ago

Fire Flame Cooking Vessel
(Ka'en Doki)

This earthenware vessel was made by the prehistoric Jomon people in Japan. Like the Great Serpent Mound (opposite), it was crafted from material that came from the earth. Its "V" shape suggests that its base was inserted into a hole in the ground to stabilize it during use. While its exact use is still a mystery, the leaping flamelike designs suggest that fire was involved. What about the shape and decoration tells you that the vessel was likely used only for special occasions, not daily cooking?

made around 2500 BCE

TRY IT OUT

NATURE AND FUNCTION

Find a tool that involves a natural element (for example, a fan for cooling air). Now draw a design that matches the element it engages.

EARTHY MATERIALS
The Jomon were one of the earliest peoples in the world to develop ceramic traditions using clay from the earth.

Birds and Flowers of the Four Seasons

These two Japanese folding screens were painted to represent the birds and flowers in a landscape as it progresses through the seasons. It moves from fall (upper right), to winter (upper left), to spring (lower left), to summer (lower right). Gold leaf (thin sheets of gold) was applied to the background in the shapes of clouds and mist. Folding screens were used in castles and palaces to bring the feeling of nature indoors; the gold illuminated the rooms by reflecting candlelight. What do these screens say about people's attitudes toward nature?

TRY IT OUT

DESIGN YOUR OWN

Create your own miniature screens by folding two legal-size sheets of paper into six panels each. Color in scenes from different seasons across them.

made in the late sixteenth century

SILVER AND GOLD
These screens were made when new silver mines were discovered in Japan. Some silver mines also produced gold, which was used to make gold leaf like the kind included here.

Cloud-Collar Pillow
with Waves

This hollow, cloud-shaped ceramic vessel, with a wave pattern incised over its body, was made in China over 1,000 years ago. It was used as a pillow! Although this may seem uncomfortable, the slight dip in the top was meant to fit the person's head, and the ceramic material kept it cool. How do you think the cloud shape and wave design are connected to sleep?

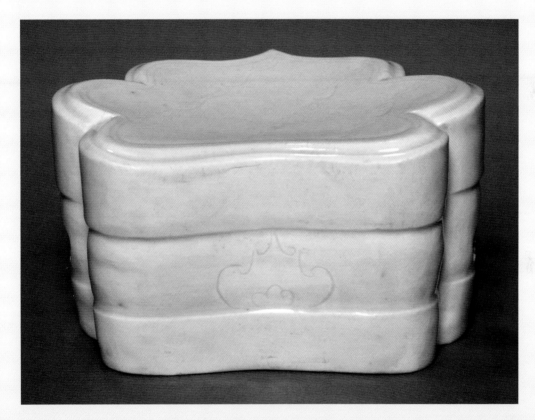

made in the 1000s–1100s CE

THINK ABOUT

NATURE INDOORS

How do the pillow and screens (like the ones opposite) use elements from nature to enhance people's experiences indoors? What desirable qualities from nature do these artworks capture?

TINTED CLOUDS
Although the pillow may look white, it's covered by a transparent (see-through) glaze with a greenish tint, nicknamed "shadow blue." How does this nickname enhance its purpose as a pillow?

Wine Jar with Fish and Aquatic Plants

This porcelain wine jar, made in China, makes you feel like you're under water! The lotus flowers and aquatic plants ripple in the wet environment and the fish swish their tails to propel themselves forward. There are four types of fish encircling the vessel's body: mackerel, whitefish, carp, and freshwater perch. When their names are recited in this sequence in Mandarin Chinese—*qing bai ling jie*—they form the phrase "honest and incorruptible" (not easily tricked into bad behavior). Why do you think this would be depicted on this kind of vessel?

made in the
1300s CE

 TRY IT OUT

COMPLETE THE SCENE

Here the side of the jar with the carp is shown. Find pictures of the three other fish and draw what you think the other three sides of the wine jar might look like.

BODY LANGUAGE
How does the jar's shape indicate where you should place your hands to carry it?

Lion Cub

This lion cub figurine was made in Egypt over 5,000 years ago, but it still sparkles like new! Carved out of quartz crystal (a hard rock that's difficult to work with), the sculpture just hints at the forms of the cub's body. Lacking a pedestal (base) and small enough to fit into your palm, it was likely meant to be touched and held rather than just displayed. What do its handheld qualities suggest about its purpose?

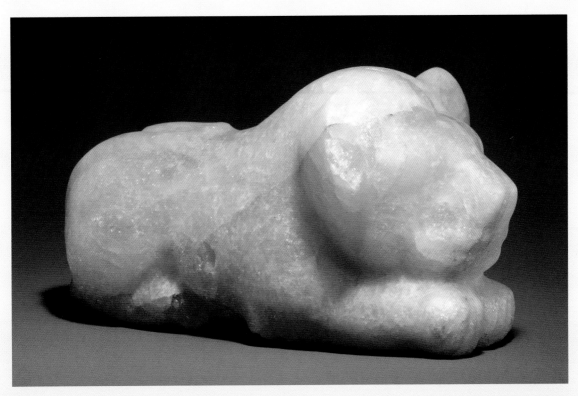

made around 3100–2900 BCE

THINK ABOUT

CREATURE COMFORTS

What do the lion cub and wine jar (opposite) say about people's desire to be close to creatures? How do these objects fulfill that desire?

FIT FOR A GODDESS
This figurine was found in a temple dedicated to the ancient Egyptian goddess Hathor, mother to the god of the sky and the sun god. How might it relate to motherhood?

Berndnaut Smilde,
Nimbus Installations

Imagine seeing a cloud indoors! Photographer Berndnaut Smilde (*BERN-howt SHMIL-duh*) uses a smoke machine and a spray bottle that produces water vapor to create thick, fluffy clouds inside churches, warehouses, and other buildings—spaces where you wouldn't expect to see clouds. He calls the clouds "temporary sculptures" because they last just a few seconds. Only the photographs he takes record their brief existence in each location.

made in the 2010s

IMAGINE

OUTSIDE IN

If you could make art that re-creates weather indoors, what kind would you choose—a thunderstorm, a gentle rain shower, a rainbow, a blizzard? What conditions would you need to produce that weather?

CLIMATE CONTROL
Although the artist can create the clouds, he can't control the shapes they make, so he often goes through the process hundreds of times until the cloud turns out just the way he wants it.

North Wind Mask
(Negakfok)

This Yup'ik mask uses wood, paint, and feathers to represent Negakfok, the spirit of the north wind. During ceremonies in winter, costumed dancers transformed into the spirits represented by their masks. Their performances were meant to keep the right balance between humans, animals, and the spirit world. Negakfok loves cold, stormy, and snowy weather. Which details in the mask help the performer bring these elements to life?

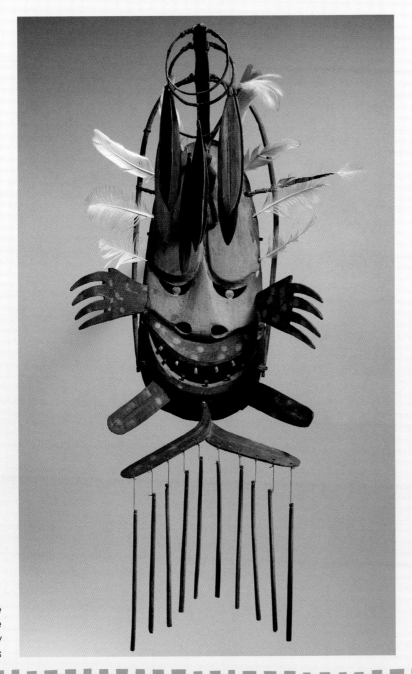

made in the early 1900s

TRY IT OUT

WEATHER MASK

If you were performing as the spirit of your favorite type of weather, what colors, designs, and textures would your mask have? What sounds would it create?

WIND CHIME
The vertical wooden sticks at the bottom of the mask jostle each other when the performer moves, creating the sounds of blustery winter wind.

Wenzel Friedrich, *Fancy Chair No. 7*

This armchair is attributed to Wenzel Friedrich. The legs, arms, and back are composed of cow horns, while the seat is covered in the fur of an ocelot (a type of wildcat). Wenzel introduced this type of furniture to San Antonio, Texas, where longhorn cattle were plentiful and wild ocelot roamed nearby. What do the chair's appearance and materials say about how some people in the region viewed nature and wildlife?

IMAGINE

HOW DOES IT FEEL?

What do you think it feels like to sit in this armchair? What activities would you do while sitting in it?

READ THE ROOM
What do you think the rest of the room that this chair is in looks like?

made after 1885

Meret Oppenheim,
Object (Le Déjeuner en fourrure)

In the 1930s, Meret Oppenheim covered an ordinary teacup, saucer, and spoon with gazelle fur to transform them into an extraordinary tea set. Although fur is usually pleasant to touch, it might feel strange to drink from a cup covered in hair or lick a fuzzy spoon! Like Wenzel Friedrich's armchair, this tea set uses nature in a way that is meant to surprise people and make them see ordinary objects from new perspectives. How does it make you feel?

made in 1936

THINK ABOUT

WILD THINGS

Many items in our everyday lives have animal patterns or are made from animal parts, such as leopard-print clothes and leather purses. How are these ordinary items different from Meret's tea set? Or are they the same?

FURRY INSPIRATION
While having lunch at a café, one of Meret's friends commented on her metal bracelet lined with fur. She responded that anything could be covered in fur, pointing to the cup and saucer on her table.

CHAPTER 6

COSMOS

The cosmos is a view of how everything in the universe is organized. It includes Earth, the sky, and outer space; all living and nonliving things; and natural phenomena such as earthquakes. Humans have continually tried to find order and meaning in the universe through creation stories, religious ideas, and scientific discoveries. Although we know a lot, much about the universe remains mysterious, sparking curiosity in scientists and artists alike.

ORIGIN STORIES

Since prehistoric times, people have observed the world and wondered how it came to exist. Why is the Earth separate from the sky? Why is there day and night? Why do the seasons change? People created origin stories to give meaning to what they observed. Some of these became part of people's religious beliefs and cultural practices, used for teaching the community where they came from, why they exist, and how to survive. Many cultures depict their creation stories in art.

Cliff Whiting, *Te wehenga o Rangi rāua ko Papa*,

made in 1974 (mural)

CREATION STORY

Cliff Whiting carved and painted this mural for a room in the National Library of New Zealand. Incorporating traditional Māori designs and materials, the mural illustrates the creation of the world and the first people.

In the beginning, Sky Father and Earth Mother were locked in an embrace. Nestled between them in darkness were their six sons. The children wanted to separate their parents so that they could enter into the world of light.

Which of the six figures do you think is the son who successfully separated his parents?

Each son tried and failed, until the sixth took his turn. Slowly, he painfully pried his parents far enough apart for light to enter the world, releasing his brothers and allowing each one to take over parts of it.

BECOMING GODS

The sons became God of Wild Foods, God of Cultivated Foods, God of Fishes and Reptiles, God of Winds and Storms, God of Forests and Land Creatures (the son who separated their parents), and God of War. There was a seventh unborn son in Earth Mother's body—he became God of Earthquakes and Volcanoes. After the sons rearranged the world, God of Forests and Land Creatures created the first people.

Giovanni di Paolo, *The Creation of the World and the Expulsion from Paradise*

In this painting, Italian artist Giovanni di Paolo (*joh-VAH-nee dee POW-loh*) shows the Christian God creating the universe. At the center is Earth, surrounded by concentric circles that represent the four elements (fire, water, earth, and air), planets, and zodiac constellations (twelve groups of stars in the sky). On the right, an angel ushers the first humans, Adam and Eve, out of the beautiful earthly garden that God created for them, because they have disobeyed orders. The four rivers of paradise lie beneath their feet, about to burst through the ground.

THINK ABOUT

HUMANS AND THE COSMOS

What does this painting say about the artist's idea of humans' role in the cosmos? How does their behavior affect their status?

made in 1445

HIDDEN HOLY FIGURES
Can you find eleven other angels in this painting? What sets the holy figures apart from the humans?

Zakariya ibn Muhammad al-Qazwini, *The Angel Ruh Holding the Celestial Spheres*

This Persian illustration, made in what is today Iran, comes from a manuscript describing the creation and ordering of the cosmos. According to the author, Zakariya al-Qazwini (*zak-kuh-REE-yah ahl-KAHZ-wee-nee*), in Islamic tradition the angel Ruh controls the positioning and movement of celestial bodies (objects in the sky). At the Creator's command, Ruh spins or stops the motion of the stars and constellations. Here, Ruh lifts up a set of concentric circles representing the planets and the four elements.

made in the sixteenth century

LOOK CLOSELY

COMPARE AND CONTRAST

Both this illustration and the painting opposite express ideas about how the universe was created and ordered. What similarities and differences do they share?

CALLIGRAPHY
The slant and shape of the calligraphy matches the clouds. Why do you think the artist did this?

Geo Soctomah Neptune, *Apikcilu Binds the Sun*

Indigenous artist Geo Soctomah Neptune (Passamaquoddy) wove this basket to depict a Wabanaki creation story that explains the existence of day and night. Envious of Sun Bird's role as provider of light, Striped Skunk tied up her wings, casting the world into perpetual darkness. The Creator sent the first human to rescue Sun Bird, but they could release only one wing. Perched atop her mountain with her other wing bound, Sun Bird casts half the world in darkness while bringing light to the other half as she slowly spins.

IMAGINE

ART IN MOTION

The basket shifts from yellow, orange, and pink to black, purple, and blue. How does this make the creation story a sensory experience?

EARTHY SCENT
Sweetgrass, a vegetable fiber that smells like hay and sweet vanilla, was used to make this basket. How might the scent make people think about their place in the cosmos?

made in 2018

Wheel of Life

Just as the basket (opposite) uses circular movement to express day and night, this hanging scroll uses a circle to symbolize life and death. Possibly made in Mongolia, the painting shows the Lord of Death clutching a wheel representing the Buddhist idea that all living things must go through reincarnation—a cycle of birth, death, and rebirth. Depending on how a being behaves in their current life, their status in the next life can improve or worsen. The sections illustrate various states and realms a being might inhabit as they go through the cycle.

made in the nineteenth century

THINK ABOUT

BELIEF AND BEHAVIOR

How can believing in reincarnation affect a person's behavior and actions?

SYMBOLIC ANIMALS
The pig, snake, and rooster symbolize ignorance, anger, and desire—emotions that Buddhism teaches are the causes of suffering. What do you think?

STARGAZING

In the 1960s and 1970s, the Apollo space missions sent humans to the moon. For the first time, astronauts were able to take close-up photos, collect lunar rock samples, and set foot on the moon's surface. Color television shared these events and images with the public. Inspired by the expeditions, Alma Thomas created this painting, capturing her excitement and wonder.

CELESTIAL WONDER

People have always been fascinated by celestial activities. We track the movement of the sun, moon, and stars. We gather to watch auroras, eclipses, and meteor showers. We give names and stories to constellations and planets. With the invention of telescopes, rockets, and space shuttles, humans have been able not only to learn about outer space but to actually go there. Art shows that our interest in astronomy (the study of outer space) is tied to our astonishment at its beauty and mystery.

SPACE ABSTRACTION

The painting is **abstract**, meaning that it doesn't depict objects and events as they appear, but instead focuses on basic colors, shapes, and designs. Here, the artist applied similar-size strokes of paint, which are slightly varied in shape, leaving bits of the white canvas uncovered to give the painting a shimmering, flickering effect. What parts of the space missions do you think are represented by her painting?

To make an abstract picture, tear up colored construction paper into small pieces and glue them onto a blank sheet of paper to represent something you see. How does making something abstract help you see things differently?

In Greek mythology, Apollo is a god who carries the sun in his chariot and guides it across the sky each day. How does this relate to the space missions and this painting?

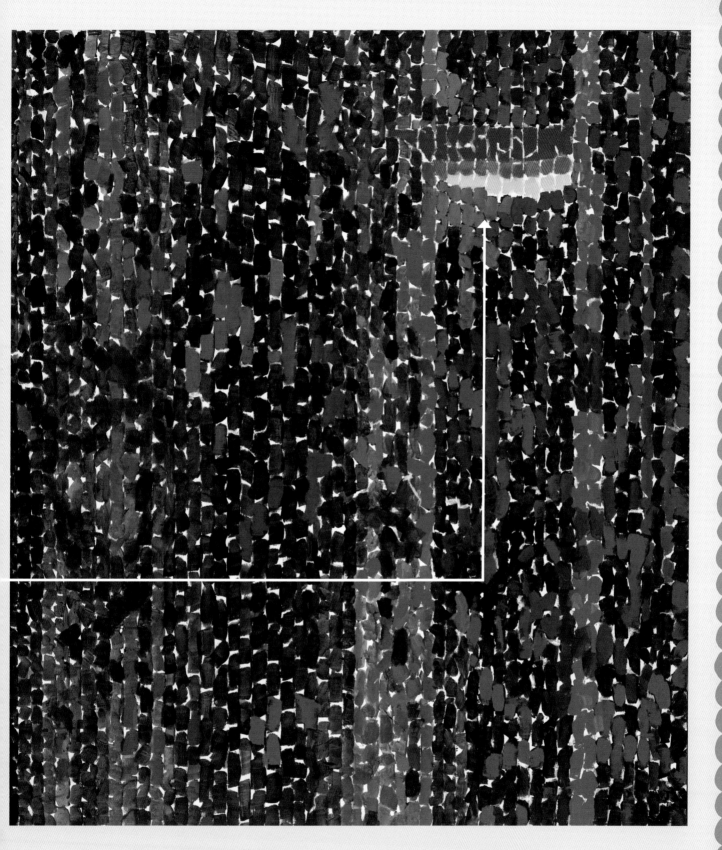

Alma Thomas, *Starry Night and the Astronauts,*

made in 1972 (acrylic on canvas)

Ellen Harding Baker, *Solar System Quilt*

Ellen Harding Baker embroidered the solar system onto a quilt and used it to teach. Although she based the design on illustrations from astronomy books, she also studied celestial phenomena (rare or significant events) in person. In 1874, she traveled to Chicago to view sunspots and a comet through a telescope installed for public use. The shimmering fin shape in the upper left is Coggia's comet, one of the objects she saw. The hairpin loop surrounding it was the path the comet traveled. Can you identify other celestial bodies in the quilt?

made in 1876

THINK ABOUT

CURIOUS QUILT

Why do you think the artist made this quilt to teach with rather than simply using illustrations from astronomy books?

SEW WHAT?
What letters and words are sewn onto the quilt? Why do you think these were added?

Joseph Wright of Derby, *A Philosopher Giving a Lecture on the Orrery*

This painting by Joseph Wright of Derby shows a group of children and adults surrounding an orrery, a mechanical model of the solar system that demonstrates the positions of planets and moons as they orbit the sun. Like the quilt (opposite), the orrery was used as a teaching tool. A gas lamp was placed in the position of the sun to replicate a solar eclipse.

made around 1763–65

 # LOOK CLOSELY

LIGHTEN UP!

The light from the lamp not only represents the sun, it also makes people's faces visible. How is each person responding to the lesson? What do their different ages and reactions say about their interest in astronomy?

SOLAR SYSTEM ART
Both the quilt (opposite) and the orrery were creative tools for teaching about the solar system. Can you create your own teachable solar system using what you have at home?

Margaret Nazon,
Night Sky

Gwich'in First Nation artist Margaret Nazon lives in the Northwest Territories of Canada, where long winter nights make the sky vivid. Inspired by childhood memories of gazing at the sky and recent images captured by the Hubble Space Telescope, Margaret sewed beaded designs of planets, constellations, and galaxies onto black cloth. The materials include glass, wood, and stone beads, as well as shell and animal bone. The different textures make the designs twinkle like the night sky.

made in 2021

 TRY IT OUT

TOUCH ART

Margaret enjoys running her fingers across the beadwork because it feels soothing. Make your own art with materials that feel good to your touch.

SIZE AND SCALE
The artist uses tiny beads to represent vast galaxies. How can using small materials to represent something gigantic affect your feelings about your own size and power in the universe?

Cosmic Cliffs

The James Webb Space Telescope has powerful cameras that capture images of outer space. This image shows a cavity within the Carina Nebula, a giant cloud of dust and gas where baby stars are formed. Young stars are extremely hot and energetic, releasing radiation that can sculpt the surrounding gas and dust into shapes that look like cliffs, mountains, and rocky pillars. These images help scientists learn more about how stars and galaxies are formed, but they also stun viewers with their dazzling beauty.

taken in 2022

THINK ABOUT

FAMILIAR AND UNFAMILIAR

What parts of this image remind you of Earth? What seems out of this world? Why do you think the scientists gave the image a title that includes a common landscape form?

SPACE ART
Create your own celestial design by gluing buttons, gems, glitter, or other craft materials onto black construction paper.

COSMIC IMAGINATION

Scientists are constantly making discoveries about outer space, but there's still so much we don't know! Are there alien life-forms on other planets? Will humans one day live in outer space? What will the future be like? Not having the answers can make us feel uncertain, but it can also motivate us to imagine exciting possibilities. Using both the knowledge humans have and the mysteries about space that are still unsolved, artists produce fun, imaginative, exhilarating works that shape how we think and feel about the future.

WINDOW TO THE UNIVERSE

In 2010, artist Kiki Smith and **architect** Deborah Gans designed a round stained-glass window for the east wall of the Museum at Eldridge Street in New York City. At the center is a six-pointed star surrounded by six arcs that span a blue background filled with gold and silver stars. The background is made up of overlapping layers of leaf-shaped glass, giving the window a glimmering, constantly moving effect. As the light outside changes, the window appears like a view of a galaxy spinning in outer space.

OLD MEETS NEW

The Eldridge Street Synagogue was built over a hundred years ago as a place of learning and worship. Today it's also a museum and cultural center where people reflect on how the past, present, and future are connected. How do you think the cosmic view in this window influences visitors' thinking about the future? How might it make people think about the passage of time?

If you were to design a futuristic window, what would it look like and where would you install it? How would you want it to affect people's feelings about the future and outer space?

**Kiki Smith (artist) and Deborah Gans (architect),
Rose Window, Eldridge Street Synagogue,** made in 2010 (glass and silicon)

Hugh Ferriss,
Philosophy

In 1929, architect Hugh Ferriss published a book filled with his illustrations of real and imagined city structures. This illustration features a futuristic city at night. The soft, blurry outlines and misty atmosphere give the scene a dreamy quality. He added people to the foreground to indicate how immense the buildings are. Visible in the sky are planets and moons, appearing much larger and closer than they would ever appear on Earth. How does this make you feel about humanity's future in outer space?

IMAGINE

CITY PLANNING

What do you imagine the tall tower and the domed structure would be used for? Why do you think the artist added trees and a pool in the foreground?

ARCHITECT OF THE FUTURE
Draw a picture of a city on another planet, including the kinds of buildings and infrastructure that humans would need.

made in 19:

Wangechi Mutu,
In Two Canoe

Kenyan-born artist Wangechi Mutu creates paintings, sculptures, and collages that feature futuristic, otherworldly spaces and beings. In this bronze sculpture, which is designed to function as a water fountain, two humanoid (humanlike) beings have their heads covered in leafy masks and limbs that extend into the ground like roots. They sit facing each other in a canoe filled with water. The artist intentionally creates art that makes viewers feel both comfort and fear. Which parts of this sculpture make you feel comfort, and which parts make you feel fear?

made in 2022

THINK ABOUT

HUMAN AND ALIEN

In art, movies, and books about outer space, there are often aliens or robots that have humanlike features or behavior. Why do you think that is?

PLANETARY ECOSYSTEM
Based on the body features of these two creatures, can you describe what their ecosystem is like? What might their planet look like?

GLOSSARY

abstract: not showing people, objects, or events exactly as they appear, but instead focusing on basic colors, shapes, and designs.

architect: a person who designs buildings.

art historian: a person who studies the various kinds of art humans have created through different periods in history.

bird's-eye view: a view of a landscape or scene from high above, as if you were seeing it from a bird's perspective, looking down.

calligraphy: decorative writing.

embroidery: decorative sewing.

frontal position: a view of a person or object from the front.

geometric: made of lines, curves, and/or shapes like circles or squares.

hieroglyphs: a type of writing that is made up of symbols and small pictures.

infrastructure: built structures that make a town or city habitable for humans; includes roads, bridges, dams, plumbing systems for water and sewage, and transportation systems.

ivory: a hard white material used for carving that comes from the long teeth (tusks) of large animals like elephants, walruses, and whales.

kaolinite: a fine white clay mineral used for making porcelain objects that are hard and solid.

kiln: an oven used for heating up clay sculptures and vessels into solids.

landmark: a building, monument, or sculpture that is well-known and easy to find in a landscape.

lithograph: a print that's made by first using a greasy crayon to draw an image onto a flat stone, then applying chemicals to the stone that attract or repeal greasy ink.

loom: a tool used to weave yarn or thread into fabric.

manuscript: a very old book written by hand, rather than typed or printed.

maulstick: a long stick used by an artist to prop up their arm and keep it steady while drawing or painting.

mica: a shiny mineral dust.

mixed media: when an artist uses many types of materials and techniques in an artwork.

mosaic: a picture or pattern made by arranging small pieces of colored stone or glass on a surface.

palette: a thin board on which an artist lays out and mixes different colors of paint; the range of colors an artist uses in an artwork.

pattern: a shape or design that is repeated.

porcelain: a hard white material made by heating up a fine white clay mineral called kaolinite; it is used for making dishes, plates, vases, and other vessels.

print: an artwork created by copying a design or picture originally drawn, etched, or carved onto a block of wood, metal plate, or stone slab.

profile: a side view of a person or object.

self-fashioning (or self-expression): when a person makes decisions about what they wear or how they look.

self-portrait: art that a person makes to represent themselves.

tapestry: a heavy cloth that has patterns, designs, or scenes woven into it.

terra-cotta: clay that has been heated up to become a hard, reddish-brown material; used for making sculptures and vessels.

textiles: cloth or woven materials that are used for clothing, rugs, curtains, or furniture coverings.

woodblock print: a print created by copying a design or picture carved onto a block of wood.

worm's-eye view: a view of a scene or the sky from a very low perspective on the ground, as if you were a worm looking up at the world.

INDEX

Words in **bold** are explained in the Glossary on pages 140–141

A

abstract 130–131, 140

Agrippina Landing at Brundisium with the Ashes of Germanicus (Benjamin West) 76, 82

Akbar (Basawan and Dharmdas) 107

Animals by the watering hole (Ali Seliem) 100–101

A Philosopher Giving a Lecture on the Orrery (Joseph Wright of Derby) 122, 133

Apikcilu Binds the Sun (Geo Soctomah Neptune) 128

architect 136, 138, 140

art historian 11, 140

Attending the Raslila (Maharana Jagat Singh) 56, 71

B

Basawan and Dharmdas, Akbar 107

Bayeux Tapestry 70

Birds and Flowers of the Four Seasons 114

bird's-eye view 71, 140

black-and-white photographs 27, 30, 38, 41, 75, 80–81

Bowl with Children in a Garden 53

C

calligraphy 64, 127, 140

Cloud-Collar Pillow with Waves 115

Colosseum, Rome 85

Cosmic Cliffs (James Webb Space Telescope) 135

Coty L'Aimant (perfume) 29

D

Dancing at the Louvre (Faith Ringgold) 66

Dancing Lesson (Raphael Soyer) 67

E

Ear Ornaments with Winged Runners, Pair of 31

Earth's Creation (Emily Kame Kngwarreye) 105

Egypt, ancient 18, 36–37, 117

Embroidered Coverlet (Colcha) (Doña Rosa Solís y Menéndez) 51

embroidery 51, 62, 140

F

Family Portrait, II (Florine Stettheimer) 40

family portraits 36–41, 67

Fancy Chair No. 7 (Wenzel Friedrich) 120

Figurine of a Girl with a Mirror (Greek sculpture) 17

Fire Flame Cooking Vessel (Ka'en Doki) 113

Four Children Playing a Game (Wade Sanzo) 47

frontal position 68–69, 140

Funerary Relief of a Vegetable Vendor (terra-cotta sculpture) 74

G

games and competitions 47, 72–73

geometric 25, 140

Grandma Moses Goes to the Big City (Grandma Moses) 98, 108

Great Mosque of Djenné, Mali 84

Great Serpent Mound, Peebles, Ohio 112

Guanyin of the Southern Sea 32

H

hair comb 19

Handle Spout Vessel with Relief Depicting a Standing Figure, Holding Farming Tools 54

Headdress (Chi Wara) 63

He Was Meant for All Things to Meet (Amy Sherald) 27

hieroglyphs 36–37, 140

House Altar Showing Akhenaten, Nefertiti, and Three of Their Daughters 37

House Model 42–43

I

infrastructure 86

In Two Canoe (Wangechi Mutu) 139

Indigenous 112, 128

ivory 19, 73, 140

J

Julie Louise Le Brun Looking in a Mirror (Elisabeth Louise Vigée Le Brun) 16

K

kaolinite 53, 140

kiln 17, 140

L

Lady Jean (George Bellows) 24

Laila and Majnun in School (Nizami) 64

landmark 84, 90, 140

Leonardo da Vinci 66

Lion Cub 117

lithograph 58–59, 140

Little Children on a Bicycle (Ernest Zacharevic) 96

Little Girl in a Blue Armchair (Mary Cassatt) 45

Little Island, New York City 92

locket 30

loom 47, 140

Lumphini Park, Bangkok 93

M

Machu Picchu, Peru 89
Maize God Emerging from a
    Flower 102
Malibu Mug (Sam Buganski) 55
manuscript 64, 127, 140
masks 106, 119
maulstick 22, 140
Medusa 17
mica 14, 140
mirrors 14–18
*Miss Harrison's Sweet Shop: House
    of Nectar* (John Heywood) 75
Mississippi Mud (Morgain Bailey) 109
mixed media 66, 140
Moche objects 26, 31, 54
Model of a Ballgame with
    Spectators 72
Moore, Harry T. and Harriette 30
mosaic 31, 140

N

*Naniwa Okita Admiring Herself in a
    Mirror* (Kitagawa Utamaro) 15
Night Sky (Margaret Nazon) 134
Nimbus Installations (Berndnaut
    Smilde) 118
North Wind Mask (Negakfok) 119

O

Object (Le Déjeuner en fourrure)
    (Meret Oppenheim) 121

P

palette 22, 140
Panel (from a Settee) 86–87
Panel from a Casket with Scenes
    from Courtly Romances 73
*Parade, from One-Hundred Views
    of Chicago* (Bronislaw Bak) 83
Parein Biscuit Tin 50
Parks, Rosa 28
pattern 24, 141
perfume 29
Philosophy (Hugh Ferriss) 138
photographs, black-and-white 27,
    30, 38, 41, 75, 80–81
porcelain 53, 141
Portable City: Hangzhou (Yin
    Xiuzhen) 90

*Portrait of Asia-Imani, Gabriella-
    Esnae, and Kaya Palmer* (Kehinde
    Wiley) 34, 39
Portrait of Mnonja (Mickalene
    Thomas) 33
Portrait of the Situ Family 38
Portrait Vessel of a Ruler 26
print 14, 141
profile 68–69, 141

R

reflection 14–15, 18
Rose Window, Eldridge Street
    Synagogue (Kiki Smith and
    Deborah Gans) 136–137

S

Sampler (Martha Perkins) 62
Seated Adult and Youth (clay
    sculpture) 60
self-fashioning (self-expression)
    20–23, 141
self-portrait 20–23, 33, 141
Self-Portrait (Judith Leyster) 23
Self-Portrait at the Easel
    (Sofonisba Anguissola) 22
*Self-Portrait Dedicated to Dr.
    Eloesser* (Frida Kahlo) 12, 20–21
Shibam, Yemen 88
shoes 11
Si-o-se-pol (Allahverdi Khan
    Bridge), Isfahan 95
Situ family 38
Sleeping Lady 44
"Smiling" Figure 25
Solar System Quilt (Ellen Harding
    Baker) 132
sportswear 27
Starfield Library, Seoul 65
Starry Night and the Astronauts
    (Alma Thomas) 130–131
Storage-Rack Panel
    (Zizwezenyanga Qwabe) 68–69
Stravinsky Fountain (Jean Tinguely
    and Niki de Saint Phalle) 94
Students Aspire (Elizabeth Catlett)
    97
Subway Riders (Ralph Fasanella)
    78–79

*Sudden Shower over Shin-Ōhashi
    Bridge and Atake* (Utagawa
    Hiroshige) 104

T

tapestry 100, 141
terra-cotta 17, 74, 141
Te wehenga o Rangi rāua ko Papa
    (Cliff Whiting) 124–25
textiles 26, 46, 47, 100, 141
*The Angel Ruh Holding the
    Celestial Spheres* (Zakariya ibn
    Muhammad al-Qazwini) 127
The Banjo Lesson (Henry Ossawa
    Tanner) 61
*The Creation of the World and
    the Expulsion from Paradise*
    (Giovanni di Paolo) 126
The Lawrence Tree (Georgia
    O'Keeffe) 103
The People Work—Evening
    (Benton Spruance) 81
The Piano Lesson (Romare
    Bearden) 58–59
The Yellow Shawl (Pierre Bonnard)
    46
Toy Kitchen 48–49

U

Unsettled Nostalgia (Mohamad
    Hafez) 91
Untitled (Gordon Parks) 80

V

Vase (Thomas Jerome Wheatley)
    110–111

W

Wedding Day, Harlem (James Van
    Der Zee) 41
Wheel of Life 129
Wine Jar with Fish and Aquatic
    Plants 116
Winged Victory of Samothrace 9
woodblock print 14–15, 104, 141
worktable 52
worm's-eye view 103, 141

Y

Yup'ik (Alaskan) mask 106, 119

CREDITS

Every effort has been made to trace the copyright holders and obtain their permission for the use of copyrighted material. If application is made in writing to the publisher, any omissions or errors will be included in future editions.

Acknowledgments

I wish to express my boundless gratitude to William Khoury-Hanold for helping me see daily the beauty that's all around. Not a day goes by that I don't feel humbled by the love and support of the extended Situ Family; their actions demonstrate to me the gift of collective care.

I owe immense thanks to Edward S. Cooke for teaching me to think about objects in new and diverse ways. My appreciation extends to the countless young people who have shared with me their perspectives on art over the years; they've opened my eyes to see how fun and wondrous the world can be.

Much respect goes to this book's project team at Quarto and Union Square & Co.: Ruth Patrick, Elinor Ward, Beth Dymond, Ardyce Alspach, Sarah Bell, Martina Calvio, Sally Bond, Caroline West, and Nic Nicholas. Their diligence and attention made this project a pleasure to work on.

I dedicate this book to its young readers: May they see beauty in this world, and may it inspire them to create more to help heal its broken spaces.